# THE GREEK ISLANDS

Genius Loci

*View of Naxos island seen through the monumental doorway of the Archaic temple.*
Thomas Hope (1769-1831)   Watercolour, 44 x 29 cm.   Benaki Museum, Inv. No. 27375.

## Author's acknowledgements

This series of twenty books covering the Aegean Islands is the fruit of many years of solitary dedication to a job difficult to accomplish given the extent of the subject matter and the geography involved. My belief throughout has been that only what is seen with the eyes can trustfully be written about; and to that end I have attempted to walk, ride, drive, climb, sail and swim these Islands in order to inspect everything talked about here. There will be errors in this text inevitably for which, although working in good faith, I alone am responsible. Notwithstanding, I am confident that these are the best, most clearly explanatory and most comprehensive artistic accounts currently available of this vibrant and historically dense corner of the Mediterranean.

Professor Robin Barber, author of the last, general, *Blue Guide to Greece* (based in turn on Stuart Rossiter's masterful text of the 1960s), has been very generous with support and help; and I am also particularly indebted to Charles Arnold for meticulously researched factual data on the Islands and for his support throughout this project. I could not have asked for a more saintly and helpful editor, corrector and indexer than Judy Tither. Efi Stathopoulou, Peter Cocconi, Marc René de Montalembert, Valentina Ivancich, William Forrester and Geoffrey Cox have all given invaluable help; and I owe a large debt of gratitude to John and Jay Rendall for serial hospitality and encouragement. For companionship on many journeys, I would like to thank a number of dear friends: Graziella Seferiades, Ivan Tabares, Matthew Kidd, Martin Leon, my group of Louisianan friends, and my brother Iain— all of whose different reactions to and passions for Greece have been a constant inspiration.

This work is dedicated with admiration and deep affection to Ivan de Jesus Tabares-Valencia who, though a native of the distant Andes mountains, from the start understood the profound spiritual appeal of the Aegean world.

McGILCHRIST'S GREEK ISLANDS

# 8. NAXOS
## & THE LESSER CYCLADES

GENIUS LOCI PUBLICATIONS
London

McGilchrist's Greek Islands Naxos and the Lesser Cyclades
First edition

Published by Genius Loci Publications
54 Eccleston Road, London W13 0RL

Nigel McGilchrist © 2010
Nigel McGilchrist has asserted his moral rights.

ISBN 978-1-907859-08-3

A CIP catalogue record of this book is available from the British Library.

The author and publisher cannot accept responsibility or liability for
information contained herein, this being in some cases difficult to verify
and subject to change.

Layout and copy-editing by Judy Tither

Cover design by Kate Buckle

Maps and plans by Nick Hill Design

Printed and bound in Great Britain by TJ International Ltd, Padstow, Cornwall

The island maps in this series are based on the cartography of
Terrain Maps
Karneadou 4, 106 75 Athens, Greece
T: +30 210 609 5759, Fx: +30 210 609 5859
terrain@terrainmaps.gr
www.terrainmaps.gr

This book is one of twenty which comprise the complete, detailed
manuscript which the author prepared for the *Blue Guide: Greece,
the Aegean Islands* (2010), and on which the *Blue Guide* was
based. Some of this text therefore appears in the *Blue Guide*.

# CONTENTS

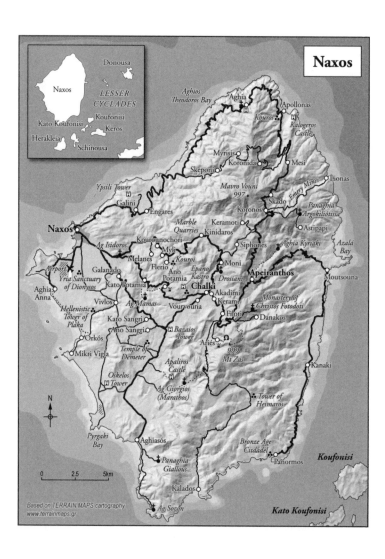

# NAXOS

Largest of all the Cyclades islands and with the highest peaks of the group, Naxos is the central, geographical hub around which they all cluster. Although not the administrative capital, it is the most important island of the group and in many ways the key to understanding the others. It has a patrimony of history, archaeology and monuments which puts it amongst the three or four artistically richest islands in the Aegean.

Because it has always been well watered, well forested, well endowed with minerals, and with a spacious, fertile interior, the island has tended to stand out amongst the other Cyclades which, by comparison, often suffered serious deficiencies of water or had little fertile land. Today it still offers the grandest and most varied landscapes in the Cyclades. Although its forests are gone—apart from some groves of immemorial oaks around Mount Zas—it is still rich in water, and its tranquil spring-fed orchards and olive groves in the heart of the island considerably modify our customary picture of the dry 'Cycladic landscape'. The striking beauty of this central garden of the island is further enhanced by the numerous Byzantine stone churches dotted among the trees, dating from the

6th to the 16th century, and mostly decorated with paintings of great quality and unforgettable presence. They are
so many in number that even this guide has had to resort
to discussing only a selection. They speak of a prosperity
on the island, especially in the period after the settling of
a tolerant Venetian dominion on Naxos in 1207. But most
of all they are the product of the island's undying sense
of its importance as a small realm of civilisation in the
middle of the sea.

The fascination of Naxos, however, is not just that it
possesses ancient remains and painted churches in great
numbers, but that the particular nature of the ruins and
churches is so unusual and instructive. The extraordinary, unfinished 6th century BC statues, lying in their
rock-cradles in the hills of Naxos, are a treasure-house of
information about early sculptural techniques precisely
because we catch them as 'work in progress'; the temples
at Gyroulas, at Yria and the 'Portara' reveal, in their ruined or incomplete state, the very turning of the wheels in
the evolution of architectural ideas. Through these monuments we come to experience vicariously the problems
and the ambitious solutions of the ancient artists and
builders. Similarly, the icons in Chora and the painted
Byzantine churches are of such variety that they are like a
history of eastern religious painting in miniature—from

Romanising beginnings, through the struggles and un-
certainties of Iconcoclasm, to the constellation of humble
talents with quite diverse artistic personalities and capa-
bilities who worked in these tiny rural chapels in the 13th
century. Naxos moves and instructs, where other islands
may just 'show'.

Development in the last few decades, especially around
Chora, has been pursued without great care, and much of
modern Naxos is an unfitting appendix to its great history. Fortunately it is such a spacious island that it has
areas, as large as counties, that still preserve a traditional
and rural island atmosphere, with far flung corners which
are quite undisturbed. And even in the heart of the tourist
areas of Chora, there are surprises; the Tziblakis cheese-
shop, functioning since 1938, is still an Aladdin's cave of
Naxiot produce, the like of which it is hard to find elsewhere—honeys, different types of sheep's cheeses, oils,
herbs, dried fruits, olives, Kitron, Tsipouro, and wines
worthy of the name of the island's patron divinity—Dionysos.

## LEGEND AND HISTORY

### Legend

Zeus himself is associated with the island, not just in name—Mount Zas, and the former name of the island, '*Dia*'—but by a tradition relating that it was on the island's peak that an eagle gave him the gift of thunder. Above all it is his son, Dionysos, who is most closely connected with Naxos and remained the island's presiding spirit throughout Antiquity. In one version he was committed as an infant by Zeus to the care of nymphs on Mount Koronos and grew up in a cave there.      It was also on a journey to Naxos that the Tyrrhenian pirates or sailors of his boat, not recognising the god, planned to kidnap him and sell him in the slave-markets of Asia. Dionysos turned their oars into serpents, immobilised the boat with riggings of vine leaves, and filled the air with the sound of invisible flutes—so greatly frightening the sailors, that they leapt overboard and drowned. The island is best known, however, from the story of Theseus's leaving of Ariadne on Naxos (*see below*) while on their way back from Crete to Athens. Dionysos found her abandoned and grieving, conceived a love for her, and had a number of children by her. The story is celebrated in one of the most accomplished poems of Catullus, in a masterpiece by Titian, and in an unusual opera by Richard Strauss.

## History

Throughout the Bronze Age, Naxos played a leading role in Cycladic culture. This had been preceded by a strong Neolithic presence on the island, both in the heights of the interior—in the cave of Zas (c. 750m a.s.l.)—and by the shore. Although there were many Early Cycladic settlements scattered around the island, as is indicated by the great number of cemeteries, the only one to survive vigorously and continuously throughout the Bronze Age was the substantial settlement at Grotta on the north shore of today's city of Naxos. This remained the island's main trading centre throughout later Mycenaean times, and it preserved enough population and momentum to survive the difficult centuries after the destruction of the Mycenaean world. In the 8th century BC, Naxos planted a (homonymous) colony in Sicily, and one on Amorgos (Arkesine). The island was never divided into city-states but constituted a single state, with its city on the site of the present town.

Because of its wealth of natural resources the island entered the historic period in a position of advantage. 'Naxos was the richest island in the Aegean' (Herodotus V, 29). Its deposits of fine sculptural marble and emery (see below), together with the fertility of its interior, meant that it was able to dominate the Ionian group of islands and their sacred centre at Delos. The 6th century BC sees a remarkable flourishing of marble sculpting and building in which Naxos, together with Samos, led the Greek world in innovative technique and designs in both areas; evidence can be seen of this in the grand monuments built by the Naxians both on the island itself, and at Delphi and on Delos. In 536 BC a civil war resulted in the overthrow of the landowning class and the instating of a tyrant, Lydgamis—himself an aristocrat, but a champion of the lower classes. In this period some of the island's most signal monuments were raised. Lygdamis was overthrown in 524 BC, and after a brief oligarchy, democracy was established. In 506 BC the island successfully withstood a four-month siege by Aristagoras, Tyrant of Miletus, supported by a group of disaffected Naxiot oligarchs in exile. At the end of the century the island was at the peak of its power and influence: Herodotus suggests (V, 30) that Naxos could raise an army of 8,000 hoplites, in addition to the fleet it possessed.

Naxos's 'golden age' ended with the Persian Wars. The island was devastated and its sanctuaries burnt by the Persians in 490 BC. It nonetheless fielded four ships to join the Greek fleet at Salamis in 480 BC, and fought at the Battle of Plataea. In 479 BC it joined the Delian League, but it was not long before it began to feel the oppressive hegemony of Athens and, recalling its own former power and glory, it attempted to secede in 473/2 BC. The Athenians firmly put down the revolt, subjugated the island, settled 1,000 clerurchs, and imposed a heavy annual tribute. Naxos never again regained its former status. In 377 BC, in the straits between Paros and Naxos, the Athenians routed the Spartan fleet with whom Naxos was then allied, and the island was forced once again to capitulate to Athens. In 338 BC the island came under Macedonian rule, then Ptolemaic rule, and finally under the Romans in 41 BC, who used it as a place of exile.

Saracen raids in the 7th century AD, forced the abandonment of the coastal settlements; but the island had a large enough interior which was agriculturally self-sufficient to remain unscathed. The surprising number of

important churches of the 6th–9th centuries with decorations—some with strictly abstract designs dating from
the period of the Iconoclastic debate—suggests that there
was a quality of life on Naxos not known elsewhere in the
Cyclades in the same period. Historical documentation is
exiguous, however, for the period of Byzantine dominion.
In 1207, in the aftermath of the Fourth Crusade, the island
was taken by the nephew of Doge Enrico Dandolo, Marco
Sanudo (*see below*) who established a Venetian 'duchy of
the archipelago' based in Naxos. The extraordinary renaissance of church building and decorating on the island in
the 13th century is ample testimony of the prosperity and
security that this brought. His descendents, and the suc-
ceeding dynasty of the Crispi, ruled over Naxos and the
Cyclades for 360 years. In 1537, Khaireddin Barbarossa
attacked, but failed to take, the island; but in 1566 Naxos
finally fell to the forces of Sultan Selim II. An Ottoman
governor was installed, but the island was never settled
by Turks. Between 1770 and 1774 Naxos was occupied by
the Russians, during the first Russo-Turkish War. Much of
the island's population, perhaps still in thrall to a Latin
culture, was lukewarm in enthusiasm for Greek Independence, expelling the Greek representatives from the island

in 1824. In 1832, however, Naxos became part of the Greek State. Italian forces occupied the island in 1941. It was liberated in 1944.

*The guide to the island has been divided into five sections, one of which is a geographical gazetteer of the 41 principal Byzantine churches which are mentioned in the text:*

- *The Chora of Naxos*
- *A gazetteer of Byzantine churches on Naxos*
- *Central and southwestern Naxos*
- *Northern Naxos*
- *Apeiranthos and eastern Naxos*

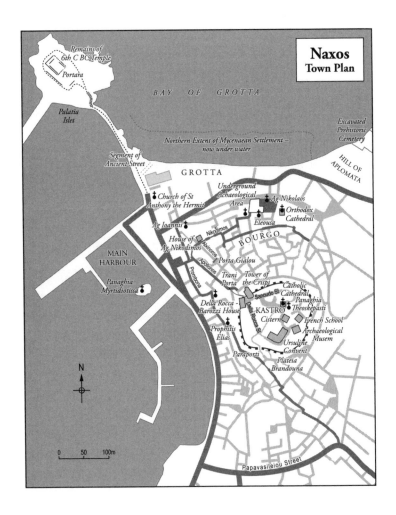

**Naxos**
Town Plan

Remains of
6th C BC Temple
Portara

Palatia
Islet

BAY  OF  GROTTA

Excavated
Prehistoric
Cemetery

Northern Extent of Mycenaean Settlement –
now under water

HILL OF
APLOMATA

Segment of
Ancient Street

GROTTA

Church of St
Anthony the Hermit

Underground
Archaeological
Area

Ag Nikolaos

Orthodox
Cathedral

Ag Ioannis

Nikodimos

Eleousa

House of
Ag Nikodimos

Akinaos

BOURGO

Porta Gialou

MAIN
HARBOUR

Prombora

Apollonos

Panaghia
Myrtidiotissa

Trani
Porta

Tower of
the Crispi

Catholic
Cathedral

Sanoudo St

Della Rocca -
Barozzi House

KASTRO

Panaghia
Theoskepasti

Cistern

French School

Della Rocca St

Prophitis
Elias

Archaeological
Musem

Ursuline
Convent

Paraporti

Plateia
Brandouna

N

0    50    100m

Papavasileiou Street

# THE CHORA OF NAXOS

From the arriving boat, the salient outlines of the history of Naxos are visible at a glance. In the distance, high on the mountains of the interior behind the Chora, are the white scars of the modern marble quarries on whose predecessors the island's early history depended, making it the first and foremost centre for monumental sculpture work in the Aegean; to left, on its enisled hill, stands the great marble frame of the 'Portara', the surviving doorway of what would have been the biggest temple in the Cyclades if it had ever been completed, and whose ambitious size is a measure of the importance and self-esteem of the island in its heyday of the 6th century BC; ahead is the hill of the Venetian *Kastro*, with its attractive cascade of buildings inside and outside its walls—symbol of more than three centuries of Venetian, Catholic domination of the island which was to bring Naxos protection and wealth in the difficult years of the Late Middle Ages. In recent decades the city has expanded in all directions, covering the fields that once encompassed the *Kastro*. In the process the building work has revealed important evidence of yet another period in which the island was preeminent: throughout the Bronze Age, Naxos was a flourishing and important centre, based around the Bay of Grotta on the city's northern shore.

The shape of the modern harbour has been considerably altered: on the north side of the main modern mole, prostrate columns and blocks of marble can be seen breaking the water surface. These are what remains of the moles, built in 1207 by Marco Sanudo, the first Venetian overlord of the island, and constructed with 'debris', including columns and architrave blocks garnered from dismantling the Portara temple and other monuments. The small chapel of the **Panaghia Myrtidiótissa** (which appears to float in the southeast corner of the harbour) sits on part of these constructions: its common name among islanders—the 'islet of Bacchus'—suggests that the church may replace a shrine to Dionysos on the same site. A number of columns and architectural fragments lie on its platform.

At the north end of the waterfront are some trees in the middle of which stands the bronze statue of Petros Protopapadakis (1854–1922) from Apeiranthos on Naxos, who was prime minister at the denouement of the Greco-Turkish War in 1922. After the catastrophe of the Greek defeat at Smyrna, he was arrested by a revolutionary military committee, convicted of high treason in the so-called 'Trial of the Six', and summarily executed.

One block in from the waterfront, the atmosphere changes from a tawdry commercialism to a more traditional island tranquillity which prevails in the network of narrow stepped alleyways around the base of the hill. Frequently, fragments of antiquity are encountered: many of the churches and a number of the house-entrances have door-frames composed of fine ancient blocks. A short climb from the southeastern end of the small plateia which extends back from the waterfront, the alleyway passes through its own 'Portara'—a small marble gateway constructed of ancient blocks with a carved lintel still bearing square dowel-holes, at the foot of Alxinoros Street. This is generally known as the '**Porta Gialou**'. Similarly, the door-frame of the venerable church beyond the northeast corner of the plateia, at the beginning of the old market street, is a composition of ancient architraves and thresholds.

The old town divides into two appreciably different areas; the Venetian *Kastro* on the hill above; and the Greek '*Bourgo*' around its circumference, stretching as far as the north shore—at which point it becomes the area of *Grotta* which is covered under a separate section below.

## KASTRO

The *Kastro* occupies the roughly circular summit of the
Prehistoric, Classical and Byzantine acropolis. The principal entrance is in the northwest corner where the steps
rise steeply beneath the most substantial remaining segment of the **13th century Venetian enceinte** of fortifications, which visibly includes many blocks of ancient
marble in its construction. Projecting bulkily to the north
is the only remaining example of the many fortified towers in the walls of Marco Sanudo's original enceinte; it is
known both as 'Sanudo's Tower', and as the '**Tower of the
Crispi**', who were the last family of Venetian overlords of
the island. Its interior exhibits a small collection of Early
Christian and Byzantine sculptures.

### MARCO SANUDO

How old Marco Sanudo was when he joined his non-
agenarian uncle, Enrico Dandolo, Doge of Venice,
in the expedition against Constantinople in 1204,
is not known since there are no documents record-
ing his date of birth. But he was well positioned, and
with courage, charm and shrewdness enough to take
full advantage of the scenarios which the capture of

Constantinople opened up. The partition agreement between the conquerors of the city assigned the Cyclades, Sporades and Dodecanese, as well as the Ionian islands in the Adriatic, to Venice. But Venice did not possess at this point the financial and human resources necessary to conquer and hold such a disparate territorial empire, although it devoutly desired the trading privileges and freedom of the waters that went with it. So it was happy to 'lease out' or delegate lands and rights to individuals—provided that they were of good Venetian families and loyal to the mother city and her commercial interests. Sanudo stepped into this role. Fitting out a fleet at his own expense, together with other like-minded adventurers, he set out to take the Cyclades—a private enterprise, undertaken on the plea of suppressing piracy and restoring order to the waters. Most of the 17 islands he took put up little resistance: the plague of piracy and raiding in the Aegean was so great that anyone who gave promise, as Sanudo did, of some degree of protection against them was willingly accepted. Only Naxos resisted because it was currently held by a group of Genoese mercenaries. In 1207

Sanudo landed near modern-day Aghiasós and, in an act characteristic of his personality, burnt his boats so that there could be no turning back. Five weeks later he had taken the stronghold of Apaliros Castle from the Genoese, and the island, indeed the whole western Aegean, was thenceforth his domain. He proclaimed himself Duke of Naxos with allegiance primarily to the Latin Emperor in Constantinople rather to than Venice, was later recognised as Duke 'of the Archipelago' (the word is an Italian corruption of the Greek, Αἰγαίον πέλαγος, 'Aegean sea') and built his capital on the acropolis of Naxos. Keeping Paros, Milos, Syros and the islands closest to Naxos for himself, he 'leased' the others as fiefs to his companions in arms, in much the same way as Venice had dispensed the islands to him: Andros to the Dandolo family, Tinos, Mykonos and the Sporades to the Ghisi, Keos and Seriphos to the Giustiniani, Santorini to the Barozzi, Astypalaia to the Querini, and Anafi to the Foscolo families.

Courageous and fortunate in adventure, he was also tolerant and intelligent in the exercise of power, attracting loyalty from those below him. Ambition, or perhaps mere injudiciousness, however, led him into two failed enterprises: first an attempt in 1212 to seize Crete for himself from the Venetian Governor whom he had ostensibly set out to help; and then in 1213, to attack the Byzantine Emperor, Theodore Laskaris, now in exile in Nicaea. Though the enterprises failed, what is interesting and instructive about Sanudo's character is how he emerged from these two escapades: the Venetian Republic apparently bore him no serious resentment for his disloyalty in Crete; and, through his charm, intelligence and attractive personality, he won back not just his freedom from the Emperor Theodore, but the hand of his sister in marriage.

Sanudo was now married to a Greek aristocrat; and his son, Angelo, was bi-lingual. He became thereby a prominent example of cultural and religious tolerance. And that in turn became a model for the peaceful co-existence of Orthodoxy and Catholicism, of Greek with Italian. The Cyclades have been notable for an absence of religious bigotry: Orthodoxy was never suppressed or harried, and to this day there are large Roman Catholic communities in the islands.

Perhaps for this reason, more than for any other, his duchy survived through twenty successors and three and a half centuries, presiding over a remarkable prosperity and a flourishing of art in Naxos in the 13th and 14th centuries. Sanudo died in 1227.

Ahead is the finely constructed Gothic arch of the main gate, or '**Trani Porta**': a vertical incision (82cm long) on the right-hand marble post of the entrance-arch marks the standard Venetian measure or 'yard', for the pricing of merchants' cloth. Inside the Trani Gate, the **house of the Della Rocca-Barozzi** family is immediately to the right, now a small museum (*open daily 10–2.30, 4.30–9*).

The Della Rocca family, whose origins were Burgundian (de la Roche), styled themselves Dukes of Athens from 1207 to 1308; and the Venetian Barozzi family was given the lordship of Santorini by Marco Sanudo in 1207. The building has remained in the possession of the intermarried families continuously: it was their city residence, and was supplemented by fortified towers in the rural interior of the island which were also the property of the family. The rooms are pleasingly proportioned and luminous for a fortified dwelling. There is a variety of kinds of ceiling, ranging from the

Venetian '*cassettone*' (main room), to the traditional island wattle over cypress beams, sealed with seaweed and sand-mud for insulation (chapel). The fine doors, in a beautiful native Naxiot cedar-wood (now no longer produced on the island), are surmounted with escutcheons and endowed with ingenious locking mechanisms which allow time for escape through a trap-door in case of surprise attack. Within the substantial thickness of the walls on the west side is a minuscule escape route, communicating with adjacent buildings. The spacious storage-cellars now host a programme of concerts in the summer.

Both south along the curve of Della Rocca Street and up Sanoudou Street to the left are many stately Venetian residences: some bear the family's coats of arms, carved in stone above the entrance—an ostentatious practice that was frowned upon back home in Venice. Among them is the residence of the Sommaripa family, barons of Paros through the 15th and 16th centuries. The atmosphere in the *Kastro* was always one of a rarified Catholic aristocracy, separated physically and culturally from the native, Orthodox Greek inhabitants over whom it ruled. The focus of this world was the **Roman Catholic Cathedral of the Presentation of the Virgin** at the summit to the east (*open daily 10–1.30, and during liturgies*).

Although some scholars maintain that this was built originally by Marco Sanudo in the early 13th century as a Catholic place of worship, it is more likely to have been adapted
from a pre-existing Byzantine basilica: this would better
explain its curious hybrid design—a basilica with a central
dome over an inscribed cross, with no apse. The structure
has been rebuilt once and restored twice over the intervening centuries: the façade was rather clumsily re-clad in
Naxiot marble in the last century. The escutcheons over the
door are of the della Craspere, Crispi and Sanudo families
(from left to right), with that of the (?)Venetian Republic
inserted second from the right. East of the crossing are two
antique columns, one of which is fluted; their capitals have
vestiges of their 17th century colouration. On the north side,
in places, the floor is laid with elaborate memorial stones
commemorating the dead of the many grand Italian and
French families who still inhabited the *kastro* in the 16th,
17th and 18th centuries: there were once many more me-
morials. Above the altar, in an ornate 17th century frame, is
the magnificent, full-length *icon of the **Virgin and Child**
with the figure of the donor below—an Italianising processional icon of the late 13th century of consummate beauty.
The icon stands a serene 190cm high. By the Virgin's feet
kneels the donor, Bishop John of Nicomedia, with a prayer
to the Virgin written just above him. The rear side bears the

figure of St. John the Baptist (*ask the attendant to turn the icon*). Along the east wall are a number of interesting paintings of the 18th and 19th centuries—most notably the panel dedicated to St Carlo Borromeo with scenes of his life. In the south aisle is a delicate 17th century, *Virgin of the Rosary*.

In the small church of the **Panaghia Theosképasti**, directly to the east of the Catholic cathedral, are two more particularly fine *****icons**, both dating from the 14th century: the *Virgin 'Hodeghetria'* with a powerful *Crucifixion* on its reverse, and the damaged icon of *Aghia Anastasia*.

The brilliant marble façades and paving of the streets within the *kastro* underscore the slight lifelessness of the area; although they constitute an ensemble of grand and historic buildings, the human presence among them is lacking. To the south of the cathedral are the lower remains of the central tower of the original, 13th century fortress of Marco Sanudo—now used as a water cistern. To its east stands the residence of the Catholic bishop, and beyond it, the buildings of the **Ursuline Monastery** and its school which functioned for 300 years from its founding in 1672 until it was closed in 1973. Off the small square formed by these buildings is the entrance to the **Naxos Archaeology Museum** (*open daily except Mon 8.30–3.*). Although displayed somewhat dowdily and with patchy labelling, its importance lies particularly in its wide-ranging and magnificent collection of Cycladic, marble figurines and objects.

(*Main floor*) The small collection of **Neolithic** finds, includes (*case to right of door*) a small **strip of beaten gold**, perforated at the corners—the oldest gold artefact to be found in the Cyclades—dating from the 4th millennium BC, which was found along with copper tools and other objects in the Cave of Zas just below the highest summit on the island, indicating contacts with North Aegean centres (?Macedonia) far from this inland Cycladic site.

The **Cycladic artefacts** dating from the late 4th and 3rd millennia BC are created from local marble, shaped with obsidian from Milos, and then extensively refined and finished by abrasion with the island's abundant emery. The dignified forms of the **marble bowls** and offering platters are satisfyingly simple, but, without metal tools, these were arduous to create. The interior of a bowl or jar—once the exterior had been painstakingly shaped by rubbing with emery—had to be hollowed out by making countless laborious perforations with a wooden drill tipped with obsidian, then connecting the perforations into a continuous cut by abrading and chipping the residual material between them, removing a core, and then further abrading and enlarging the interior. Given the time-consuming difficulty of all this, it is remarkable that the pieces emerge in so masterfully symmetrical and pure form. Similar technical processes were used with the *figurines (*show-cases in first room*). These vary in height between 20 and 50cm: the majority are of female figures, most commonly with arms folded, narrow shoulders and relatively large necks and heads, bearing a sculpted nose but no other facial features: this is the typical 'Spedos' type, named after the finds from Spedos in southeastern Naxos. From the cemetery of Louros in southern Naxos comes an even purer and more schematic form, without arms—the so-called 'Louros' type. Of particular beauty are the several examples of **seated female figures**, with arms crossed, on stools or high-backed 'thrones' (mid 3rd millennium BC), whose proportions tend towards the naturalistic. Once again the lack of arms, rather than distracting, in fact enhances concentration on the volumes of the body. Contemporary with these pieces are a number of objects in clay which have survived: a **zöomorphic cup** in the form of a pig (*right hand wall*), and a set of **wide-rimmed bowls**, like up-turned hats.

Subsequent rooms exhibit objects from the **Mycenaean** burial sites on Naxos, which have yielded fine jewellery and bronze ornaments—including a series of small **gold sheets**

**with framed and embossed figures of children** (*middle gallery*). In the cases against the walls are other examples, with repoussé forms of lions, bull's heads and other animals, found at Aplomata and at Kamini. A frequent design on the decorated Mycenaean pottery is the sensuous and fluid octopus motif—symbol of regeneration. One of the most unusual pieces is a vase (*third gallery*) **decorated with two moulded snakes** whose heads drink beside its spout. Note also a small **12th century BC *hydria*** bearing an unusual scene of fishermen drawing in a net with its catch; and the fragments of a large *pithos*, decorated in relief with chariots and riders who bear Homeric, 'figure-of eight' shields. The fine col-

lection of Geometric vases comes from the cemeteries at Tsikalarió on Naxos and at Vathy Limenari (*see p. 170*) on Donousa. Amongst them are the burnt remains of fruits and nuts which were given as offerings.

(*Mezzanine floor beyond galleries.*) The collection of Archaic exhibits is small for an island with such artistic preeminence in the period. They include a fine **6th century BC, *kouros* head** from Grotta, and fragments with bold Archaic inscriptions—including a disc-like grave-marker with clearly inscribed border. At the edge of the *outside terrace* are two **unfinished Archaic kouroi**—one almost life-size, the other substantially smaller. In the centre of the terrace is displayed an ornate but unsophisticated **mosaic** of the 3rd or 4th century AD, figuring a marine nymph, framed by corner-segments with peacocks and hinds, which was found in a late Antique house in Naxos. Of note among the other Hellenistic and Roman exhibits (*final room, upper floor*) is a large collection of beautiful **Roman glass**.

The museum adjoins the former **French School** whose main building is down the alley to the left, as you face the museum entrance. Founded in 1627 with a charter approved by both the Pope (Urban VIII) and the Ottoman Sultan (Murat IV), and open to Catholic and Orthodox students alike, it became one of the foremost schools of the Aegean world. The novelist, Nikos Kazantzakis studied here as a boy in 1896, until—as he relates (with some elaboration) in his *Report to Greco* (1961)—he was forcibly removed by his father and returned to Crete.

The street (named after Kazantzakis) leading out of the West Gate or '**Paraporti**' of the *Kastro* winds down past a series of grand residences with refined marble ornamentations to their window and door frames, as far as the small esplanade of Plateia Brandouna, which is lined with cafés and tavernas, and offers cool on summer evenings and views over the port towards Paros.

## BOURGO

The oldest surviving church in *Bourgo*—the lower part of Chora—was built probably in the late 13th century, if the distinctive armorial bearings with the four Bs of the Palaiologos family, placed over the door, can be taken as relating to its founding and early patronage: formerly known as the Panaghia *Vlacherniótissa*, it is now the church of Prophitis Elias, one block in from the waterfront at the level of the Emporiki Bank. Inside the church are two particularly beautiful, 15th century icons by Angelos of Crete—a painter of great refinement and elegance who may have influenced the early Venetian painters, such as Pietro Veneziano, and in whose tradition El Greco was trained a century later.

At the northern extremity of the waterfront, before the causeway to the 'Portara', is the 15th century church of **St Antony the Hermit**, built by Duchess Francesca Crispo and gifted to the Knights Hospitaller of St John in 1452. It must have been an isolated church outside the habitation at first, because the heart of the *Bourgo* clung closely to the north and western slopes of the *Kastro*.

The principal thoroughfare—at times scarcely wide enough for two people to pass—which runs east from the waterfront, often under the projecting upper floors of buildings, is **Nikodimos Street**, named after the island's patron saint, Aghios Nikodimos of the Holy Mountain (1749–1809), whose house can still be seen (third doorway on the left after the 'Taverna Vassilis') beyond the sharp turn east in the street.

Nikodimos was born on Naxos, studied in Smyrna and spent much of his adult life on Mount Athos, where he became one of the most influential teachers and writers of Greek Orthodoxy during the years of the Ottoman occupation. He was much influenced by the Hesychast tradition of contemplative mysticism, and was the person who first compiled and published the teachings of the early ascetics in a highly important five-volume work known as the *Philokalia*. He wrote widely on spiritual practice and prayer, and translated some important Italian Jesuit writings into Greek. He was canonised in the Orthodox Church in 1955: his feast on 14 July is the island's principal celebration.

Nikodimos Street eventually debouches into Mitropoleos Square, an open, low-lying area dotted with churches which surround the **Orthodox Cathedral of the Zöodochos Pigí**, built in 1786 on the site of an earlier church. The interior is dominated by an impressive **marble iconostasis**, contemporary with the church's construction:

the grand icon of the *Virgin, as Fount of Life,* with its carved unified frame is also of the same date. The dome is supported on antique columns. The arresting, but rather crudely carved funerary slab of the Venetian nobleman, Niccolo dalle Carceri, is set into the floor of the entrance portico.

Because of the dominant position of the Roman Catholic Venetian community in Naxos, the early Orthodox churches in the town tended to be simple and unadorned: the wealth of Byzantine pictorial and architectural display, on the other hand, was concentrated almost exclusively in the Orthodox heartland of rural Naxos. After the Venetians lost their control of the island to the Turks, many of the earlier churches in this area were pulled down and rebuilt. The square is surrounded by churches and chapels but none has any special decoration and all date from the 18th century: to the west is the Panaghia Chrysopolítissa, with three contiguous chapels dedicated to the Apostles, and SS. Spyridon and Charalambos; to the south is the Panagia Eleousa; and to the north Aghios Nikolaos, which lies at a lower level because it is built on the base of a previous church of clearly considerable antiquity. To the east of this area of town lived the Jewish community but the whereabouts of the Synagogue is not known. At the opposite western end of the square is the monument and (rapidly eroding) marble bust of Michalis Damiralis (1857–1917), a Naxiot scholar, philologist and translator of Shakespeare whose face is depicted below on the monument. Close by it are stones and architectural fragments from the **Hellenistic and Roman agorá** of Naxos, which lay under the eastern end of this area, stretching as far as the Bay of Grotta.

## GROTTA

The **Bay of Grotta** was the site of the Bronze Age city of Naxos, which archaeologists are slowly revealing in piecemeal fashion in the midst of today's habitations. The shoreline has receded considerably and the foundations of much of the prehistoric city and the later structures built over it now lie under water in the bay. Aerial photography shows clearly where a long, roughly rectangular shelf of building and wall foundations extends 10–15m out to sea, and stretches for much of the length of the bay. At the neck of the causeway to 'Palatía', to the east side, just before the first buildings of the town, can be seen a **segment of uncovered ancient street** (running at right angles to the axis of the causeway): this would have communicated between the ancient north and south shores.

The area of **Grotta** represents an important cradle of Cycladic civilisation. Its history is complex, however: hence a word of general introduction to the finds displayed here.

## NAXOS TOWN IN PREHISTORIC TIMES AND AFTER

### Neolithic and Early Cycladic Naxos
(This period is best appreciated through a visit to the Archaeology Museum.)

Excavations carried out at the western end of Grotta Bay ('Kokkinovrachos') showed that the later levels of habitation in the area lay over a Neolithic settlement of the mid-5th millennium BC: the finding of obsidian from Milos and pottery techniques influenced by mainland Greece shows that this was a settlement that enjoyed external contacts. It is with the 3rd millennium BC, however, that there is a 'revolution' and that the previously discontinuous pattern of Neolithic habitation is transformed into an interconnected tissue of settlements which are found all over the Aegean islands. This change is perhaps as much the result of advances in sea-transportation as it is of improvements in agricultural technique and management. Populations suddenly increase and settlements acquire social organisation. We know more about this period from burials than from anything else because of the perishable nature of the domestic building. The graves were shallow cists lined and covered with flagstones in which the body was buried with the knees drawn up to the chin. The richer graves typically contain pottery and marble vessels, jewellery and bronze weapons: but of their contents, it is the small marble figurines which have spoken most eloquently of this distant period to the popular imagination. These make a pronounced debut at many different points on Naxos—mainly because of the abundance of excellent marble and of emery with which to smooth it, while the relative proximity of Milos made obsidian for fashioning the marble available. One of the finest examples is the small figurine of a female figure sitting on a high-backed throne dating from c. 2500 BC (*Naxos Museum*). This was found in the cemetery on the hill of Aplómata, visible at the eastern end of the bay.

Following the upheavals at the close of the Early Bronze Age, of which we have ample evidence from all around the Aegean area, the populations of the many flourishing Cycladic settlements were radically reduced: most of the smaller ones were abandoned and the population seems to have concentrated in a few of the most strategically secure places. Grotta became in this period the most important—if not the only—large settlement on Naxos. And by the 15th century BC its art and culture began to have a pronounced Mycenaean accent.

## Mycenaean Naxos (1300–1050 BC)

(This is best appreciated through a visit to the excavations beneath Mitropoleos Square.)

The Mycenaean city of Naxos lay along the bay of Grotta and incorporated the island of Palatía to the west; its cemeteries were on the hill of Aplomata to the east; and it covered the area between the submerged shoreline to the north and the acropolis hill to the south. It appears to have developed in two distinct phases: first, a smaller city of the 14th century BC which was probably destroyed by earthquake around 1250 BC; in the next phase, this was overbuilt by a second city, oriented differently, which developed and grew continuously until about 1050 BC. This second city was enclosed with a fortification wall in the second half of the 13th century BC, in the face of some clearly present threat. The method of construction of the walls was unusual: a broad base or socle of uncut stones, surmounted by ramparts in mud-brick, similar to the early walls at Kolona on Aegina. Once again, from the funerary and other finds that have been made on the cemetery hill of Aplomata and at Kamini, it would appear that Mycenaean Naxos was a prosperous city with extensive trading links with Cyprus, Egypt and with the mainland of Greece. With the destruction of the Mycenaean palaces on the mainland, the trade networks and commerce on which Naxos depended, with its central and strategic position in the Aegean, began to diminish. The low lying area seems to have been abandoned in the face of threat from the sea, and the rump population retreated to the higher and safer ground of the acropolis citadel.

## An unusual continuity into Historic times

The walls and ruins of the Mycenaean city remained visible above ground after the abandonment of the area. Its descendents, who now inhabited the hill of Kastro, venerated these ruins and created, with the passage of time, a cult around their grand ancestors whose world now began to appear 'heroic' to them. They buried their own dead in the previously inhabited area as a way of strengthening the links with this glorious past, and raised a tumulus on the area beside the Mycenaean fortification walls where they worshipped their ancestors as heroes. This occurred around the 8th century BC at the same time that Homer's epics were reinforcing the cult of a heroic past in the psyche of the Greeks. This was also the period in which the foundations of the new Classical city of Naxos were being laid. Its *agorá* was laid out in this area, beside the tumulus and the ruins of the Mycenaean fortifica-

tions, which remained as a focus of cult until as late as the
1st century AD, when it appears the area was finally covered
by Roman housing. The '*heröon*' or tumulus stood directly
to the north of where the Mitropolis Church now stands: the
*agorá* extended to its west and north.

The ***Mitropolis Archaeological Area** (*open daily except
Mon 8.30–3. Admission free*), entered opposite the church
of Aghios Nikolaos, is an exemplary display of what are
complex archaeological finds. The various areas and stra-
ta visibly recount the history outlined above, as well as
highlighting the decisions archaeologists have to take as
they work down from level to level through a history as
dense as this. The unusual construction of the Mycenaean
walls can clearly be seen. There are ceramic workshops
from the same period—one in which the work-bench
and drying shelves are clearly visible, and where slip-
coated pots with colour ready to be fired were found *in
situ*. At another point an exceptional, painted *krater* was
found (copy on site, original in museum). Higher up,
above these levels, can be seen Classical door-ways and a
Roman oven. There is also fascinating evidence of a cemetery *hermax*—the cairn or pile of stones left by visitors
as they exited a cemetery. It was customary to make this
symbolic and apotropaic gesture as you left the 'polluted'

area of a cemetery in antiquity, as if the stone which you threw behind you onto the *hermax*, carried away any 'pollution' or ill-omen.

On the top of the hill of **Aplomata** to the east of the bay of Grotta, excavated graves can still be seen at the seaward edge. The small marble war memorial nearby commemorates Nikolas Binikos from Ikaria, who was killed in 1944 in the struggle to oust the German occupation of the *Kastro*.

## THE 'PORTARA'

The *Portara is the most conspicuous and best-known Classical ruin on Naxos: its silhouette, standing on a small islet joined to the main island by a causeway, is visible from the town, from the port, from the mountains and from far out to sea before arriving. It is the largest constructed monolithic doorway from the Archaic period in Greece, and is the only standing element remaining from a temple built around 530 BC under the period of rule of the tyrant Lygdamis, and subsequently left uncompleted. In its scale and ambition it expresses the prosperity, confidence and technical mastery of one of the most powerful centres in the Aegean at that time. Lygdamis's Naxos in many ways rivalled Polycrates's Samos and Peisistra-

tus's Athens. All three tyrants knew one another. Naxos
had already begun to make its unmistakable mark on the
pan-Ionian sanctuary of Apollo at Delos with impressive
works of architecture and sculpture. Here, however, it was
embellishing its own front door, marking the entrance to
its harbour by what was to have been the grandest and
most visible temple in the Cyclades. The building was
neither the first nor last place of cult on this tiny islet:
Lygdamis's building was raised on the site of Early Bronze
Age structures, and there is evidence of human presence
on the islet as far back as the 4th millennium BC. Later,
through early Mediaeval times, the temple was itself occupied by a Christian basilica with an inscribed apse,
which was erected inside it, during the 6th century AD.

Debate is far from concluded as to the intended dedication and the design of the building. Long thought to
have been a sanctuary to Dionysos, patron divinity of the
island, it is now generally thought to have been a temple
to Delian Apollo, although this leaves unresolved problems relating to the unusual orientation of the building
(*see below*). It was once thought to have been designed
as a porticoed temple *in antis*, with two Ionic porches
to either end and with two rows of four columns divid-
ing the interior space into three aisles. It is now generally
believed that a much more ambitious and visually strik-

ing peripteral structure was intended, with a colonnade all around, which doubled on the short sides. Given the breadth (6m) and height (7.9m) of the existing doorway and its height off the ground, the much greater width of a peripteral design would have given the building more appropriate proportions. In this hypothesis the temple would have had 12 columns on the long side and a double row of six on the short sides, bringing the overall area to c. 55 x 37m. It is not clear whether or not there would have been an open entrance at the opposite, southeast end, either comparable in size or smaller. Nor is it clear where the altar would have been placed and therefore which way the temple faced, nor why the orientation of its main axis is so unusual.

There is an image of the Portara on the frontispiece of this book.

## The remains

What is visible on the ground conforms well with a dipteral design. The two parallel lines of meticulously cut and interlocked blocks of foundations for the walls of the *cella* (measuring c. 37m x 15.5m by 12m high) are clearly visible. The outlines of the *antae* and the distyle *pronaos* beside the portal, and of the *opisthodomos* (also distyle) at the opposite end, are both discernible. The exquisite, crystalline quality of Naxiot marble and the fine finishing of the surface of the pieces with a bronze point can be noted in the blocks which are strewn over the area. One piece near the pathway in the south corner still bears the parallel scores from the drill and peg holes made when it was quarried from the rock-face. A great many of the blocks still possess the 'knobs' on their surface, left uncut so as to provide a 'handle' to help with block-and-tackle lifting and transporting: these are particularly evident in the monoliths of the portal, where they are of very large dimensions. These would have been removed and smoothed before completion.

The configuration of the site is made harder to read by the fact that an Early Christian church (removed in the 19th century) was created within the temple's *cella* in the 6th century AD. An entrance into it from the west was cut directly through the middle of the threshold block of the portal, leaving it thenceforward sundered in two. The church's floor level was therefore well below that of the threshold block. This fact also raises a series of unknowns. Was this floor level already in existence in the design of the temple? Probably yes, for two reasons: there would have been no point or motive for the Christian builders laboriously to dig out a lower level of floor if one had not already existed and if they could have used the floor of the existing cella of the temple. Second, the marble paving to the inside of the portal appears to be contemporaneous with the temple: it may, in fact, have belonged to a lower undercroft or treasury to the building (cp. the Archaic Temple of Hera on Samos), covered by a stone or wooden floor, c 1.90m above, at the level of the threshold. If this higher floor had deteriorated or collapsed, or had never even been finished, then the Early Christian builders would have had to use the lower level of floor and to cut a new entrance through the ancient threshold and its foundation courses.

What remains today of the temple is instructive of ancient building techniques in several ways: these can be summarised as follows:

**Order of construction**. The habit—part practical, part symbolic—of laying a threshold first, followed by the door posts and lintel, and lastly building the rest of the structure around it, is as old as architecture itself. It can be seen in earliest Neolithic house-building. The door-frame here, which has proved so extraordinarily resistant through time, almost certainly came first and the other elements of the temple followed piecemeal thereafter. All other measurements and elements followed on from the main doorway once it was erected, since it is unlikely that there was a preconceived master design or comprehensive plan of measurements drawn up beforehand.

**The raising of the doorway.**      The doorway stands well above the present ground level raised on at least four courses of marble masonry acting as foundation. This extra height would have made the erecting of the verticals and the lintel much harder. How was this done? It can be seen that the profile of the hill has been cut away substantially where the temple now stands, in relation to the summit to the north. *Before* this digging away was done, the foundation courses would have been sunk deep in a trench in the hill and the threshold block put in place. At this point a mound of earth, produced by excavating the hill further back would have been built up behind (*southeast*) the trench which contained the threshold block and foundations. The massive door posts would then have been brought into position, lying on the steep slope of the mound of packed earth, with the dowels in their bottom surface in position beside the corresponding holes in the threshold block. The lintel block must then have been 'bolted' onto the door-posts so that the whole locked upper frame could then be raised from a 45 degree position to vertical, on top of the threshold, until the dowels sank satisfactorily into their holes, holding the now complete frame in perfect order—a position it has held ever since, throughout tremors and quakes in the intervening centuries.

The unresolved curiosities which the structure presents can be summarised as follows:

**Decoration**. In spite of meticulous engineering and cutting of the principal blocks, the running ridges carefully carved on the outer (northwest) faces of the blocks of the portal patently do not continue or correspond from one block to the next, leaving an awkward transition from the horizontal to the verticals, which furthermore is of a different degree of discrepancy to left and to right.

**Orientation**. Accepting the hypothesised dedication to Apollo for the moment—the majority of temples to Apollo are oriented on an east to west axis; some notable exceptions (e.g. Apollo *Epikourios* at Bassae) are on a north to south axis; here at Naxos we have a northwest/southeast axis. This is explained erroneously by some as an orientation towards Delos, the epicentre of Apollonian cult. Delos lies well to the north of northwest from here, and on a clear day it is possible to verify with the naked eye that the temple in no way 'looks towards' the sacred island. The axis of the temple *is* however perfectly aligned with the summit of the hill of the Kastro, towards which its (south)east 'front' faces. There is no epigraphic evidence to suggest whether the summit of Kastro was or was not occupied by another sanctuary in antiquity, to which the temple was in some way related.

**The 1925 curiosity**. In December 1883, Theodore Bent and his wife visited Naxos and saw the Portara: 'the two white marble doorposts and the lintel, standing up high and solitary on the summit of the little green island, a conspicuous object from everywhere'. We see it today just as they saw it then. But in a frequently reproduced photograph of 1925, the islet of Palatia is clearly visible, but there is a conspicuous and complete absence of the Portara.

Looking back to the land from the Portara, the hill of the ancient acropolis now occupied by the old town enclosed within the walls of the Venetian castle is directly ahead along the axis of the temple. The Venetians used the Portara as a quarry for large blocks of marble, and many of its elements can be seen built into the walls of the *Kastro*. The ruin has become the symbol of the island and one of the most famous landmarks in the Cyclades. Local mythology holds that it was on this tiny islet that the sleeping Ariadne woke to see her faithless lover's ship disappear over the horizon to Athens, and grieved until she was found by Dionysos.

**ARIADNE ON NAXOS**

Ariadne was the daughter of King Minos of Crete and Pasiphaë. When Theseus, prince and preeminent hero of Athens, came to Knossos in Crete as part of a human tribute of Athenian young men and virgins who were sent each year to King Minos as expiation for the death of his son Androgeus in Attica, Ariadne glimpsed him and fell in love with him. She provided him with a ball of wool with which to help him escape again from the Labyrinth once he had slain the Minotaur: as she did so, she asked Theseus to promise that he would marry her in return and take her with him when he escaped, so that she would avoid the wrath of her father. Theseus assented. After Theseus escaped successfully from the Labyrinth, having achieved his mission, the two fled north: their first stop was Naxos, then called '*Dia*'. While Ariadne slept, Theseus set sail for Athens and abandoned her: she awoke to find him gone. Dionysos, finding Ariadne grieving on Naxos and seeing her mortal beauty, fell in love with her. He presented her with a gold wreath set with precious stones; later this was placed in the heavens as the constellation of *Corona Borealis*. And

she bore him children. So—in this version of the
story at least—the god converted her grieving into
a renewed fertility, like the return of a new spring.
In Antiquity, festivals which must have originated in
relation to an 'Earth Goddess' celebrated Ariadne's
story: a mourning festival which recalled her sleep,
abandonment and almost-death from grief; and a
subsequent festival which celebrated her awakening
and marriage with Dionysos.

The story, as Plutarch recognised (*Theseus*, 20),
had many versions and there were many explanations of what Theseus was up to. Homer implies that
Ariadne was already married to Dionysos when she
followed Theseus from Crete, and that she was killed
on *Dia* by Artemis at the request of Dionysos. Anacreon, Apollonius of Rhodes and Hyginus say that
she bore Dionysos sons: Anacreon says one, Apollonius four, Hyginus six. Diodorus and Pausanias
claim that Theseus left Ariadne because the gods
commanded him to, since Fate would not allow him
to marry her. Ovid and Hyginus suggest Theseus was
simply a rotter. Plutarch mentions that, in some accounts, Ariadne came to Cyprus (not Naxos) already

pregnant by Theseus, who abandoned her there. And anyway, he adds, the Naxiots themselves claimed that there were in fact two different Ariadnes—one for Dionysos and another for Theseus. The story of Ariadne and Theseus encapsulates the ambivalent view that Naxos had of Athens and Athenians. History had taught Naxos not trust Athens.

## BYZANTINE CHURCHES OF NAXOS

Naxos has a greater concentration and chronological spread of mediaeval and Byzantine churches than any other Greek island, including Crete and Kythera. Amongst them are some of the oldest rural churches in the Aegean. There are more than 130 important examples—many of them painted; some with rare decorations from the Iconoclastic period of the 8th and 9th centuries; all of architectural interest. It is an extraordinary patrimony, as well as a boon to the visitor because so many of them are set in rural landscapes of great magnificence. The walks and climbs involved to seek them out are one of the joys which Naxos offers.

Naxos was large enough to possess a safe and fertile interior which was sufficiently far inland to avoid the destructive attentions of pirates and raiders: it is in this central zone of the island that most of these early churches are located. Nothing can fully account for the remarkable flourishing of ecclesiastical art in the early 13th century on Naxos. The stability brought by the establishment of a ruling Venetian dynasty partly explains the phenomenon; commercial links with Crete are also important; but the ferment of building and decorating which happened in this period goes beyond these explanations.

In the face of such a historic wealth of monuments we have divided the churches and monasteries of the island into three categories:

- the **five** most important—'**essential**'—churches on the island, whose significance or beauty is such that they should at all costs be seen while on Naxos;
- a second group of **10 important** churches, which are of interest for a variety of different reasons. The churches in both these groups are described in detail in the text;
- a further **26 worthwhile** churches of interest (most with paintings) are listed at the end, together with their whereabouts. They are organised according to area, so that they can be easily located when you are in a given part of the island.

The list is far from exhaustive.

**Access**. Opening arrangements can be a very real problem for the visitor because many churches are kept locked nowadays. A good proportion of our 15 important churches have access that is relatively easy, even if their posted opening times are not adhered to outside of the high summer months. Some are always open; some have particular hours; some may require tracking down the local priest, or *pappás*, in the nearest village to obtain the key. But for some of the most important, opening needs to be arranged through the Byzantine Antiquities Department (or Ephorate) in Chora, which is located in the Sanudo/Crispi Tower in *Kastro* (*T. 22850 22225*). Only by people continually asking to visit the churches will it become clear that there is a public interested in looking at the island's treasures. Perhaps this will lead to their greater availability. Otherwise, if an ancient church on Naxos is open, do not fail to go inside. They are always of interest and the opportunity of an open door is golden.

For the best and most detailed study of these churches, see Giorgios Mastoropoulos, *Νάξος, το ' άλλο κάλλος/Naxos: Byzantine Monuments*, Athens, 1996.

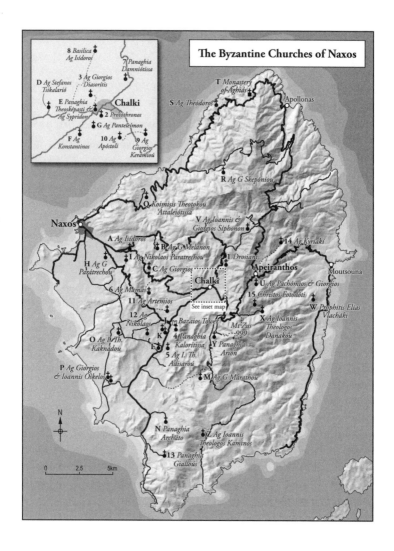

**The Byzantine Churches of Naxos**

8 Basilica
Ag Isidoros

7 Panaghia
Damniótissa

D Ag Stefanos
Tsikalarió

3 Ag Giorgios
Diasorítis

Chalki

E Panaghia
Theosképasti &
Ag Spyridon

2 Protóthronos

G Ag Panteleímon

F Ag
Konstantinos

10 Ag
Apóstoli

9 Ag
Giorgios
Keramioú

T Monastery
of Aghiás

S Ag Theódoros

Apollonas

R Ag G Skepóniou

Q Koímisis Theotokou
Attaleiótissa

V Ag Ioannis &
Giorgios Siphonon

Naxos

A Ag Isidoros

B Ag G Melanon

14 Ag Kyriaki

1 Ag Nikolaos Paratrechou

1 Drosiani

Apeiranthos

Moutsouna

H Ag G
Paratrechou

C Ag Giorgios

Chalki

U Ag Pachómios & Giorgios

6 Ag Mámas

15 Christos Fotodóti

11 Ag Artemios

See inset map

W Prophitis Elias
Vlacháki

12 Ag
Nikolaos

J Bazaios Tower

Mt Zas
·999

X Ag Ioannis
Theologos
Danakou

K

4 Panaghia
Kaloritissa

Y Panaghia
Aríon

O Ag I. Th.
Kaknádou

L

5 Ag I. Th.
Adisaroú

P Ag Giorgios
& Ioannis Oskeloí

M Ag G Marathou

N

0    2.5    5km

N Panaghia
Archáto

L Ag Ioannis
Theologos Kaminos

13 Panaghia
Gialloús

# GAZETTEER OF CHURCHES

Group I (All in **Central Naxos**): '*Essential*'.

1. *__Monastery of the Panaghia Drosiani__—6th century and later. (3.5km north of Chalkí on the road to Kinídaros. Generally kept open throughout the year from 8–1, 4–8. Offering to custodian.)

2. *__Church of the Protóthronos (Panaghia)__—6th century and later. (On the main street of Chalkí. Generally closed except for liturgies in the early morning and on Sundays: the pappás, however, is frequently to be seen in the village and will open the church.)

3. *__Aghios Giorgios Diasorítis__, mid-11th century. (1km northwest of Chalkí: signed, 10-minute walk from the main street in Chalkí along footpath. Generally open 10–2 with custodian in summer. Otherwise key with Ephorate)

4. *__Monastery of the Nativity, Kalorítissa__—7th–14th centuries. (Partially hidden, but visible, half-way up the west slope of hill of Prophitis Elias above Bazaios Tower; 30-minute climb. Outer area unlocked.)

5. *__Aghios Ioannis Theológos Adisaroú__—9th century. (In the area of Lathrina, c. 1km east of the Temple of Demeter archaeological site, in a field to the east of the Chalki/Aghiasos road, 2km south of the Bazaios Tower. Generally closed: key with Ephorate.)

Group II: '*Important*'
Near Potamiá (9km southeast of Chora)
6. *__Church of Aghios Mámas__ (or of the 'Panaghia Theosképasti'), 10th century. (25min walk from main road: take two right forks from Kato Potamiá—2km; unlocked.)*

Near Chalkí and Keramí (16km east-southeast of Chora)
7. *__Church of the Panaghia Damniótissa__ (800m northeast of Chalki: at the first curve after the end of the straight stretch of road leading to the Drosianí, the church lies 80m across olive grove to the left. Open 10–2.30.)*

8. *__Basilica of Aghios Isídoros__ (1.5km north of Chalkí, by track to north from point 600m west of the main junction in the village centre. Unlocked.)*

9 *__Church of Aghios Ioannis Theológos Keramioú__ (150m east of the main road passing through Keramí, to the north of the village centre. Track leads left from the main road-sign with the name of the village through an olive grove to the church. Open 10–2.30.)*

10. *__Church of the Aghii Apóstoli__ (250 m to the south of the main road passing through Keramí, to the west of the village centre. Path leads in the opposite direction from the same point as the path to Aghios Ioannis Theológos Keramioú (above). Locked, but exterior of greatest interest.)*

Near Sangrí (13km southeast of Chora)

11. *__Church of Aghios Artémios__ (1.5km east of Kato Sangri; visible in the valley from the Chalkí/Sangri road, c 1.5km north of the Bazaios Tower and 3km south of Chalki. Key with Ephorate.)*

12. __Church of Aghios Nikólaos__ (signed, south of Ano Sangrí. Open Mon–Fri, 10–2.30 in summer.)

Near Aghiasós (24km south of Chora)

13. __Church of the Panaghia Gialloús__ (4.5km south east of Aghiasós in the foothills to the east of the shore. Unlocked.)

Near Apeiranthos (26km east of Chora)

14. __Church of Aghia Kyriakí__ (at Kaloni) (4.5km northeast of Apeiranthos by footpath only; allow three hours to go and return. Unlocked.)

15. *__Monastery of Christos Fotodóti__, or of the Transfiguration (6.5km south of Apeiranthos, turning signed 4km before arriving in Apeiranthos. Currently open and being restored.)

Group III: 'Of interest'

Central and western Naxos

(**Itinerary (i) Chora—Melanés—Kinídaros—Moní**)

A. *Aghios Isídoros.* Beside road junction on the of main Potamiá road, 3.8km east of Chora waterfront. Always open.

B. *Aghios Giorgios Melánon*. At the foot of the village of Mé-
lanes, beside the stream-bed. Key with *pappás*.

## (Itinerary (ii) Chora—Potamiá—Chalkí—Keramí)

C. *Aghios Giorgios*. North side of the road at Kato Potamiá,
7.5km from Chora.

D. *Aghios Stefanos* at Tsikalarió. Village of Tsikalarió.

E. *Panaghia Theosképasti* and *Aghios Spyridon*, double church.
By the high school in Chalkí.

F. *Aghios Konstantinos* at Vourvouriá. 400m outside, and due
south, of village of Vouvouriá, 1km southwest of Chalkí.

G. *Aghios Panteleímon*. 500m due south of Chalkí.

## (Itinerary (iii) Chora—Galanádo—Sangrí—Bazaíos Tower—Lathrínos - Aghiasós)

H. *Aghios Giorgios Parátrechou*. South of Chora–Vivlos road,
4km east of Chora waterfront.

I. *Aghios Nikolaos Parátrechou*. Footpath north from sharp
right bend before Galanádo.

J. *Aghios Ioannis Theológos Avlonítsas*. In open country southwest of the Bazaios Tower and east of Aghios Nikolaos.

K. *Panaghia Arkouliótissa*. West of Chalkí–Aghiasós road, 1km
south of Bazaios Tower.

L. *Aghii Giorgios and Nikolaos Lathrínou*. West of Chalkí-Aghiasós road, 3km south of Bazaios Tower.

M. *Aghios Giorgios* at Upper Marathós. 3.5km south of Bazaios Tower, a track leads east towards Apaliros Castle, ending after 2km below the southwestern ascent to castle; a path for a further 3km skirts south, round the hill and climbs the valley eastwards up to Aghios Giorgios. Allow 3+ hours (return).

N. *Panaghia at Archáto*. Southeast of settlement of Archáto, 4km northeast of Aghiasós.

## (Itinerary (iv) Chora—Yria—Vívlos—Pyrgáki)

O. *Aghios Ioannis Theológos Kaknádou*. 1km down track southeast off main road, 2km south of Vivlos.

P. *Aghios Giorgios and Aghios Ioannis* at Óskelos. Just above the unmistakable Oskelos Tower, 2.5km east of Kastraki.

## Northern Naxos

Q. *Koimisis tis Theotokou Attaleiótissa*. West side of Engarés valley, north of Chora.

R. *Aghios Giorgios of Skepóni*. Village of Skepóni.

S. *Aghios Theódoros*. Behind beach of Aghios Theodoros at the northwest tip of island.

T. *Monastery of Aghiá*. In the valley below the Aghias Tower, at northern tip of island.

## Apeiranthos and eastern Naxos

U. *Aghios Pachómios* and *Aghios Giorgios*. Adjacent to one another to east, below road before entering Apeiranthos: take concrete road to right, immediately on entering habitation. *Aghios Ermolaos* lies further to east.

V *Aghios Ioannis and Aghios Giorgios of Síphones.* From junction 5.5km north of Apeiranthos, road leads south to Síphones; church visible to west, below road.

W. *Prophitis Elias Vlacháki.* 2km south of Moutsoúna, track leads west inland for 1.5km: church visible above, is reached only by footpath.

X. *Aghios Ioannis Theologos.* Village cemetery of Danakós.

Y. *Panaghia Arión.* To east of the Filoti/Heimaros Tower road, 1.7km after initial junction at Filoti; path doubles back to church in middle of field. Churches of Ag. Anastasia (2.2km) and Aghios Eustathios (3km) further south.

Z. *Aghios Ioannis Theologos Kaminos.* To west of road on hill at '*Pirniá tis Farlas*', before steep descent of road; access difficult.

## BYZANTINE ARCHITECTURE AND WALL-PAINTING ON NAXOS

At first sight, Byzantine painting can seem much of a muchness. To eyes trained in the tradition of the Western Renaissance, with its emphasis on individuality and naturalism, it can appear fossilised and repetitive. It does repeat, and was meant to repeat it is visual liturgical 'chanting'. But it is not without character, modulation and considerable range of quality. Just as in coming from daylight into a dark interior, it takes time for the eyes to adjust to its subtle inflections. First, there are chronological variations: the earliest paintings on Naxos, of the 6th and 7th centuries, (*Drosianí, Protóthronos*, and *Kalorítissa*) show the characteristics of late Roman painting—'sculpted' robes (i.e. painted with a fine sense of depth and texture), arresting gazes, a sense of vigour and urgency. In the next period of the 8th and 9th centuries, the Byzantine world was riven by the debate about whether images were a good or bad influence in sacred places: in 730, Emperor Leo III decreed the destruction of all sacred images in human form throughout the Empire. Earlier paintings were plastered over with abstract decorative works, which sometimes recall the *faux marbres* of Pompeian painting; from this period, we find only symmetric designs, as if for tiles (*Aghios Ioannis Adisaroú*, and *Aghios Artémios*), and very occasionally symbolic animals (*Aghia Kyriakí*). Once the Iconoclastic debate was over (843), and concluded in favour of the reinstating of images, there was some sober reflection followed by a renewed flourishing of religious art—which emerges as graceful, vigorous, colourful and with a just balance of space and figure. This is exemplified especially in the 13th century paintings of *Aghios Giorgios Diasorítis* and in *Aghios Nikólaos*. With the passing of this renewed energy, Byzantine painting starts to become more formal and stylised from the 15th century on: a flatness of drawing, replaces the 'sculptural feel' of earlier robes, and the faces of saints and protagonists become more elegiac; then distant; and finally vacant. The 16th and 17th centuries in Byzantine art are characterised by an emphasis on narrative content, above all else; a *horror vacui* sets in and every space is filled with detail which disperses the concentration of the image.

As well as these broad historical developments there are distinct personalities at work in the churches of Naxos. Take three cycles of paintings for example, all painted in the 12th or 13th centuries. The artist at the church of *Panaghia Galloús* has a thoughtfulness and softness of style which is quite his own. He is a naturally contemplative artist, and the tonal harmony of yellows and reds which he uses reinforces the gentleness of his big-eyed figures. This contrasts markedly with the painter in the church of the *Panaghia Damniótissa*, whose faces are unique in the horizontal elongation of their eyes, the narrow foreheads and chiselled features: in their sharply glyptic manner, his figures are not without pathos, but they belong to a quite different artistic personality. In the church of the *Protóthronos*, the painter of the *Annunciation* on the sanctuary walls (south side) reveals his sophisticated, metropolitan training in his graceful sweeping curves and ox-eyed figures with gracious brows and gestures of the hand—quite different from the highly stylised angular 'button-holing' directness of the earlier painter working on the figures in the dome of the same church. Again, in the magnificent church of *Aghios Giorgios Diasorítis*, we can distinguish two artists, in this case working at the same time (*see below*). In short, there is a considerable variety of sounds coming from this orchestra of painters, even though in the end they are all—importantly—playing the same piece of music.

What was the 'music'? The 'ideal' Byzantine church is a circle on a square: the circle, which has no beginning or end and therefore symbolises the eternal Heavenly cosmos, sits on top of the square, whose four sides symbolise the earthly world of four elements, four seasons, four cardinal points, and so forth. This gives you a dome, over a square or rectangular floor-plan; heaven over earth. The decoration of the interior was subsequently designed to reflect this symbolic symmetry: the dome depicts the heavenly panoply, while the lower walls figure the earthly life of Christ and of the saints who dwelt in the world. In the pendentives in between these two areas were to be shown the 'communicators' who bridged the gap between the two—namely the Evangelists. The earthly scenes, furthermore, were not to be seen against a bright background, but the figures instead were to glow against the darkness of our benighted ignorance. Hence the predominantly dark blue colour which customarily fills the space around the figures in Byzantine wall-paintings. Byzantine painters used a simple range of naturally occurring earth pigments. There was a spiritual symbolism to this, too: God created Man out of the 'dusts of the earth', and they—in worldly imitation of that—would create their images of man from those precious dusts of the earth which we called pigments. Commonly occurring ferric oxides provided yellows, reds and browns; though for a stronger red, Spanish cinnabar might be used. The blue was provided by azurite (naturally occurring copper carbonate) from Hungary (and not, in a remote island such as Naxos, by very expensive ultramarine or *lapis lazuli* from Afghanistan). Even azurite was expensive, and the simplest painting cycles use a black instead, made from charred vine-twigs, which has a bluish tinge to it. Azurite blue was generally mixed and modified with other colours because if used alone in high concentrations it tended to turn green in the wet caustic lime-plaster. For this reason, blue was also frequently added afterwards in tempera onto the surface of the plaster once it had dried. Another colour added '*a secco*' in tempera onto the dry surface was a pasty enamel-like lead white, used to create broken highlights on faces and the folds of garments. It is because of this mixed dry and wet technique, that we cannot truly call Byzantine wall-paintings 'frescoes'—in the sense that works by Masaccio or Michelangelo which were painted entirely into freshly-laid wet plaster are 'true fresco'. Their techniques were different, just as what they were doing in painting was also quite different.

# CENTRAL AND SOUTHWESTERN NAXOS

Four itineraries: see map (*Chora = 0.0km for distances in text.*)

## I. Chora–Melanés–Myloi/Flerio–Kinídaros–Drosianí–Chalkí (23km)

Nearly four kilometres from the harbour of Chora, a left branch off the Potamia/Chalkí road, heads east for Melanés: in the 'V' of the junction is the 13th century church of **Aghios Isídoros** (**A**), a barrel-vaulted structure with blind arcades in the interior which incorporates marble spolia from an ancient building, visible in the south and west walls, and is decorated extensively with 14th century paintings. The fine overall effect of the paintings exceeds the general quality of the workmanship, even though there are faces of occasionally great beauty. Two kilometres west of here (by immediate left branch) beyond the village of Angídia, north of the road is the site of the Early Christian basilica of **Aghios Stéfanos Frarón**, within which a later 11th century church was built. All that remains standing are fluted columns of the structure, believed to have been taken from the Temple of Hestia on Paros. Taking the main (right-hand) continuation of the road, you come to **Melanés** (8km). The church of *Aghios Giorgios Melánon* (**B**), beautifully set by a stream in the depth of the valley appears to have been built over a Late Roman structure, and the adjoining chapel on the north side converted from an ancient cistern. A beautifully inscribed fragment of cornice is immured in the exterior of the south wall. There are several layers of painting on the vault, and the north and south walls of the interior: some fragmentary graffiti-like designs dating from pre-iconoclastic times; other aniconic designs; and later 12th and 13th century layers, including a fine Pantocrator whose face has the dignity and presence of a Constantinopolitan icon. A faint Early Byzantine inscription on the north wall is the invocation of a certain 'John of Melanes'.

At **Kalamítsia**, 2km west of Melanés by unpaved track, are the atmospheric ruins of the *18th century palatial **mansion of Parátrechos**, used as a retreat by the Jesuits. The large complex of residences, chapels, byres and out-buildings are set in utter tranquillity among lush vegetation and palm-trees watered by springs. In the lowest level of the main building is the former mill-installation. The site is unexpected and beautiful—with something of the feel of an abandoned stage-set. The track descends to the main Potamiá road beyond the ruins.

### Flerio

East of Melanés is the village of Kour[ou]nochóri (6.5km), where the turreted and machicolated **Mavrogenis/Della Rocca Tower**—one of the best preserved of the several early Venetian towers in the valley—rises conspicuously above the village roof-scape. These 'towers' were fortified manors belonging to the important Venetian families of the 14th and 15th centuries, built to mark and survey their rural properties.

Just beyond, the road descends to **Flerio** (10.5km): this is the site of the two ***unfinished marble *kouroi***, which constitute one of the most fascinating remains in the Cyclades, as well as of the recently uncovered **ancient sanctuary** nearby. A path leads left from where the road ends along a plane-shaded torrent-bed, and then cuts alongside a garden of citrus trees to the right: just above the orchard, you unexpectedly come upon the first *kouros* lying in a small walled enclosure beneath some ilex trees. The sight is momentarily breath-taking. The massive supine figure, 5.8m long, is, beneath the dark patination of its surface, in pure white marble. It lies in the place where the uncut block was initially detached from the bedrock of the island. This is clear from the chiselled striations and workings of the stone in the immediate vicinity. After the piece had been given an approximate form and principal characteristics as a *kouros*—i.e. a nude, standing, heroic, male figure—it was moved through 90 degrees from the position in which it was originally roughed out. Then the piece was abandoned, never worked again and left unfinished, probably because a fault in the marble at the shins of the figure (structurally its weakest point) caused the stone to fracture, though it is not impossible that some purely external factor—an earthquake or a war—caused the work to stop, and that the fracture occurred afterwards. It still lies in the same spot where it was created, abandoned, and accidentally discovered again in 1943.

### THE UNFINISHED *KOUROI* OF NAXOS

There are three unfinished, gigantic **kouroi** statues on Naxos: two here at the site of Flerio, and one at Apóllonas, near the northern tip of the island. The latter is of an apparently bearded male figure (probably Dionysos), and dates from around 550 BC. At 10.7m long, it is by a long way the largest of the three. It lies in its quarry in the bedrock close to the sea, and has been known for a long time. The Flerio *kouroi* date most probably from a little earlier in the first half of the 6th century BC, and have come to light only recently. These objects are not just remarkable and moving sights, they are also highly instructive in what they can tell us about the way ancient sculptors worked.

**Quarry site.** The *kouroi* clearly demonstrate that, in this early period in Greece, the sculptors travelled to where the stone was, rather than the stone travelling to the sculptor's workshop. Unlike the army of stone-cutters in the centre of Ancient Rome who worked in shops beneath the Palatine hill (in what is still to this day called the *Via Marmorata*) on blocks of rough-hewn marble unloaded from barges on the Tiber and brought to their door, the early

Greek stone-cutters went to where the best marble occurred in the natural landscape and did much of their preliminary work there, on the spot. Experience and local knowledge would tell them where in the mountains the purest marble deposits were. After doing preliminary soundings with a pick in the area, they would decide on a particular pure vein in the bedrock and begin the work of mapping out the figure and releasing the roughed-out form from the living rock.

**Transportation**. This, however, left the substantial problem of transportation. The marble was in the mountains of the interior and the partly finished piece had to be got down to the sea. Massive marble objects are transportable by water, but moving them over land is difficult and risky: the marble can easily get chipped or broken even in simple moves. It is clear for all to see how particularly difficult the terrain on Naxos is: steep, rough and bolder-strewn. The 12 kilometres from Flerio down to the sea look like an insurmountably difficult journey. There is the dry bed of a stream nearby, but even allowing for Cycladic deforestation and ecological change, it could never have had enough water in it to facilitate the descent in any useful way. So, unless the Naxiots had invented a very large hot-air balloon and never told us, there seems to be no alternative to their having intended to build a 'runway', in parts made of loose marble chips, in other parts of packed earth, leading all the way over this unforgiving terrain down to the shore. Sledges, carts, ropes and a great deal of man- and animal-power were then necessary to propel and to brake the movement of the fragile monoliths. No evidence of this 'piste', however, is visible today on Naxos. In Athens a road of this nature was improvised over the 15km between the quarries on Mount Pentelicon and the Acropolis hill when the Parthenon and Propylaia and the Erechtheion were being built, but Athens had a large population and a lot of slave-power, and the Athenians were transporting such large quantities of stone over a long period that it was worth their while to invest in a runway of such length and magnitude. The slope is for the most part relatively gentle and the floor of the Attic plain is considerably more accommodating than the rocky interior of Naxos.

**Destination**. It is just possible that this laborious transportation was not actually necessary because the pieces were intended for the sanctuary which has recently been uncovered some 50–100m to the north of the abandoned *kouroi* at Flerio; but, given the nature of what has been revealed so far of this site, this seems unlikely—though not impossible. Most probably the *kouroi* would have been created for exportation to another island—as in the case of the huge, monolithic statue of Apollo which was dedicated and given by the Naxiots to the sanctuary at Delos around 600 BC.

A consonance between the dimensions of the Flerio *kouros* (5.8m) and the monumental doorway (interior measurement, 6.5m) of the Archaic temple remains of the Portara could indicate that the Flerio *kouros* was destined for the cella of the temple. It is possible that work on that temple may have been stopped at the time of the overthrow of Lygdamis in 525 BC, a timing that could correspond also to the abandonment of the two kouroi, if we accept a later date for their creation.

**Sculpting method and tools used**. The fact that

these pieces were left just as they were in mid-creation gives us a rare opportunity to look over the shoulders of the scupltors and to see how they worked. The whole surface of the Flerio *kouros* is covered in small and regular circular depressions left by the sculptors' tools. The straight chisel or bull-nosed chisel generally leaves a running groove, but the sculptor's point or 'punch' (a tool like a chisel but with a pointed end) leaves such dimple-like marks. The 'dimples' reveal that the sculptor has used a hammering stroke, perpendicular to the surface of the stone. This is a laborious way to work stone: a perpendicular stroke soon blunts a tool, which then constantly requires sharpening. These perpendicular strokes were used because the sculptors' tools were not of hard enough metal for any other method. There is a ratio between the strength of the metal tool used and the hardness of the stone to be cut which limits the angle at which the tool can be used. Bronze tools of the sort available to a stonemason of the 6th century BC were not hard enough to permit the oblique stroke of a point or flat chisel: they would tend always to skid across the surface of the stone when used obliquely.

Consequently they were used perpendicularly to the surface, dislodging small pieces of marble and leaving the indentations we see all over the surface. Iron tools, by contrast, would be hard enough to allow a more oblique stroke to cut the stone, and to create a more uniform and flatter surface. Iron, though a late arrival by comparison with bronze and copper, had been known and used in the Mediterranean since before the beginning of the 1st millennium BC: but, like all metals when they are first discovered, it was still an expensive commodity in the 6th century BC. (It had been one of the most valuable prizes offered by Achilles to the victor of the weight-throwing contest in Book 23 of the *Iliad*.) The first people to benefit from any increasing availability of iron would have been the warriors and soldiers who needed it for their weaponry: in second place of importance would have come the stone-cutters. So, it appears that bronze tools were still in use for sculpture long after the introduction of iron—just as stone tools were still used in Egypt after the arrival of bronze.

Continuing to work with old-fashioned bronze tools may also have had a good technical reason.

Marble has a strong and regular crystalline structure;
by continual striking of the surface with these perpendicular strokes, the crystalline structure begins to
break down and the surface of the marble loses its
rigidity and becomes more responsive to later, finer cutting and to abrasion with emery, as the piece
nears its completion. Sculptors call this 'bruising' the
marble. The final surface of these *kouroi* was, in any
case, left intentionally rough in order that the thin
coloured plaster-wash, which was commonly used,
had something to 'key' into on the surface when it
was applied. All these early *kouroi* were brilliantly
coloured.

**Measurements and proportions**. Of all the indentations in the surface of the *kouros*, the largest
and most worn is the navel. From this central point,
all the canonical measurements which guided the
sculptor in mapping out the body were taken: used
constantly as a fixed point of reference, it has been
worn more deeply than any other point. The distance
from the navel to the break between the legs gives us
a measurement of about 33cm (the length of a fore-
arm from knuckle to elbow). It is the same distance

from the navel to the flank; the same from the chin to the crown; twice this distance, from the navel to the sternum; twice, also from the break in the legs to the knees; and again from there to the soles of the feet; and so on. In other words, a precise received scheme of proportions governed the sculptors' work, based on a single unit of length.

**Identity**. What exactly the *kouroi* 'represent' is also the subject of debate. Of the several dozen male *kouroi* that have survived from Antiquity, there is no common key to their purpose or identity. Some are grave markers, some are votive statues; some represent divinities, others heroes, some perhaps ordinary mortals or even living athletes; few have attributes of any kind to help define them better. What they all have in common is youth and nudity. The Greek word for a sculpture was '$ἄγαλμα$'—'that which gives delight'—to the deities, to the dead, or to the living. The *kouroi* are '*agalmata*'—unchanging incarnations of beauty, hence the apparent frequency with which they are associated with Apollo. Apollo was the image in which the Greeks worshipped youth and beauty. The main Flerio *kouros* could equally be an anonymous hero or an image of Apollo. The beard of the *kouros* at Apollonas, however, precludes Apollo, and for that reason it is thought generally it would have been an image of Dionysos.

From the first *kouros* a path leads to a small cottage where it is possible to take refreshments in the shade of citrus trees. Not far beyond, a path leads diagonally up the hillside to the **second *kouros***, which lies exposed on the hillside. It is of similar dimensions, and though more eroded, was in a slightly more advanced state of completion. The front of the face has sheered off and both legs are broken at the knees. Fragments of the feet and shins lie in the area. From here it is possible to cut southwest across the fields and rejoin the stone kalderimi or mule-path which leads from Myli across the hill, south to Ano Potamiá (*35mins by foot*), arriving in the village beside its spring and taverna. It is an easy and very rewarding walk, which traverses the area where some of the earliest **surface quarries** of white marble in the Greek world were first exploited. It was probably on these slopes that the elements of the Portara and of the great Naxiot dedications on Delos were first cut and shaped.

The most recent discovery in the area of Flerio is the

**sanctuary to chthonic deities** discovered on the hillside beside the point where the asphalt road ends. The sanctuary, which has an interesting and unusual circular configuration of buildings, was probably frequented predominantly by the quarrymen and sculptors, since it stands in the heart of their work area.

The first cultic buildings here date from the 8th century BC. In the 7th century BC a rearrangement of the site was undertaken, together with the building of a new marble temple. It was characterised by a monolithic door-frame (threshold visible) which, in design, prefigured the 'Portara' and the entrances of other later Ionic temples. Damage to the building occurred resulting from an earth tremor in the 6th century, and the temple and its surrounding buildings—amongst which were a *hestiatorion*, or ritual dining area—were repaired. The survival, throughout all this, of a sacred hearth for burnt offerings suggests that the divinity worshipped was chthonic—perhaps a fertility divinity, or the giants, Otus and Ephialtes, who perished on Naxos and were honoured as protectors of quarrymen. The latter—twin sons of Poseidon—are protagonists of some of the most bizarre of all Greek myths: it was they who, having declared war on the Olympian gods, 'piled [Mt] Pelion on [Mt] Ossa' on top of Mount Olympus, and threatened to make the sea dry by filling it with mountains. They bound Ares in chains and put him in a cauldron, and declared their lusts—Otus for the virgin Artemis, Ephialtes for queen Hera. When finally killed on Naxos by a ruse excogitated by Artemis, they went to Hades, were bound to pillars with snakes, and tormented by a ceaselessly screeching owl.

## Mýli

The area of Flerio and **Mýli**, the straggling village along the valley-side to its north, is remarkably rich in springs, as the name meaning 'mills' implies. The springs were used to supply the city of Naxos from as early as the turn of the 5th century BC. This involved the construction of an ancient aqueduct, in the form mostly of a superficial, constructed gulley, almost 11km in length. At an early point of its course, a tunnel was excavated: nothing as bold as the 1km tunnel of Eupalinos of Samos through the heart of the mountain was attempted here, but even so it is a notable piece of Archaic engineering. The entrance to the tunnel, refaced in stone in Roman times, can be seen by following the stone-paved path—which begins by running parallel, and just below, the asphalt road—north round the right-hand side of the valley. The aqueduct's course, which is detectable only in occasional stretches, lay past Aghios Thalelaios, Angidia, Aghios Stefanos Fraron, and thence to the east side of the hill of *Kastro* at Chora. The path leads for several kilometres amongst walled and terraced fruit orchards, and stone houses: the sound of water running is never distant, and there are frequent cascades. It constitutes one of the island's most delightful *walks.

## Kinidaros and the Drosiani Church

The road east from Mýli climbs up into the area of the quarries which are worked today—an eerie landscape of gigantic cliffs and screes of marble, in which natural colour veins are visible in places. The principal community of the quarries is **Kinídaros** (16km), overlooking a fertile valley dotted with magnificent oaks. After Kinídaros the road descends to Moní (18.5km). The village takes its name from the *monastery of the Panaghia Drosianí* (**1**), just above a curve in the road, 1km below (*Generally kept open 8–1, 4–8*). It is one of the most important Byzantine sites in the Cyclades.

This is a church, or rather complex of chapels, whose history goes back to the late 6th or early 7th century. Dedicated to the Birth of the Virgin, it is all that remains of a monastery whose buildings once surrounded it. It is a classic example of chapels or churches 'agglutinating' organically in Byzantine architecture, suggesting in this case a funerary purpose. The original core of the church is the **decorated tri-conch at the eastern end**, which was probably built as a sepulchre-church for an important holy person: the tri-conch form, derived from the circular *martyrium*, was often used for a funerary chapel. It was a persistent belief in early Christianity that the closer you could be buried in physical distance to a holy person's tomb, the greater the benefit of that person's holiness might be on your mortal remains. Hence the construction of the first additional chapel, tucked at an uncomfortable 45 degree angle to the axis of the main church against the northwest corner of the tri-conch. Later two further chapels agglutinated yet further to the west. An aisle was then added, joining them all together in to one body along with the original tri-conch. The westernmost chapel probably came before the middle one which was then haplessly squeezed in between—the ultimate effect of this clustering being that of a group of sheep, head down, pushing towards a water-trough.

Because of their antiquity, the **paintings** at the Drosianí are of considerable importance. The 6th/7th century scene of the *Ascension* (a common funerary subject) in the east conch is attended by Apostles whose faces belong to the stylistic world of Late Roman and Early Christian mosaics. The dome is decorated (same period) with an almost unique subject matter: two busts of *Christ*, one youthful and beard-less holding the Gospel, the other holding a scroll as the 'Law-giver'—one the human, incarnate Jesus; the other, the Eternal Saviour. The inscription between the two (towards the east rim) reads: 'For the salvation of Andreas and his wife and their children'. There are other inscriptions below on the east wall beside the apse, referring to the dedication of the church. In the north conch, the face of the *Virgin 'Nikopoia'* is compelling in its intensity. She is framed by roundels with *SS. Cosmas and Damian*, as if from a Late Roman mosaic. Below, are the rhythmic gestures and processional costumes of the well-spaced figures in the *Deësis*. The carved marble *templon screen* which stands (restored) to waist height is probably also contemporaneous with the building. (Later layers of painting of the 11th to 14th centuries, which were superimposed on the present paintings in the conches have been detached and are currently awaiting a place for exhibition.) Of the tiny funerary chapels on the north side, that to the east is decorated with a *Virgin 'Platyera'*; the small 'throne' in its apse may probably have been for the display of an icon. The central chapel—the only one to have neither dome nor window—has grave loculi to left and right; the bed-rock obtrudes into the floor.

The exterior silhouette of this cluster of jostling domes, cubic drums and semicircular apses, surmounted by the belfry, is unforgettable: it is humble Byzantine architecture at its most plastic.

Beyond the Drosianí the road descends to Chalkí, where it joins the itinerary below.

## II. Chora—Potamiá—Epano Kastro/Tsikalarió—Chalkí—Filóti (20km)

The valley of Potamiá is the confluence of several springs, and its upper reach is a sequence of burgeoning orchards, mills and plane-trees. The village itself straggles almost 2km down-stream from the main spring at Ano Potamiá. Coming from the port, the village begins as the valley first begins to narrow at **Kato Potamiá**, 7.5km southeast of Chora. At this point, the church of **Aghios Giorgios (C)**, with large areas of 13th century painting, lies just to the north of the road. To the south of the same point, a road descends, crosses the watercourse, and continues southwards as a rough track for a further 2km as far as the impressive ruined church of ***Aghios Mámas**, or of the 'Panaghia Theosképasti'(**6**). This is one of the most romantic ruins in Naxos, lying in a fertile valley, surrounded by mountains on the horizon: the summit at Epano Kastro is visible through the collapsed eastern vault.

When it was built in the 10th century, this was one of the largest and most important churches on the island, and may at one point have been the seat of the Metropolitan in the 11th and 12th centuries. The dedication to St Mámas, who was the protector of shepherds, is appropriate to the deeply rural setting far from the sight and ravages of pirates. The church is of an elegant and spacious, domed, cross-in-square design. There are finely carved fragments of **5th century BC, marble cornice with palmette design**, visible over the south door, and immured to north and south of the sanctuary. Other pieces of Ancient masonry and some Early Christian mullions suggest that the building had predecessors on the site or in the area. The belfry and double-vaulted narthex were added probably in the 13th or 14th century—the latter entered either from the church or from a doorway-like aperture in the west wall which is almost impractically high because of the steeply sloping terrain. Above the church to the west is an impressive abandoned house, with fine gateway and cistern.

Between **Mési Potamiá** and Ano Potamiá (10.5km), instead of following the road, it is particularly worth navigating the network of paths that border the stream bed. The route runs through orchards of pomegranate trees, small weirs, and at one point passes the 16th century '**pyrgos**' **and mill-house** of the Venetian Cocco family which, although abandoned, still preserves its beautifully carved door-frames. The mill-machinery is also still *in situ*. At **Ano Potamia**, a **spring** of excellent water flows year-round and is the origin of the dense vegetation of the valley. Beside it is one of the best tavernas on Naxos.

### Epano Kastro

As the road climbs up from Ano Potamia, the rocky height of **Epano Kastro** comes into view to the east (*left*). The castle can be approached from this side along a path signed from the road, or else from the east—from Tsikalarió which lies 5km further on (*45 minutes' climb by either route*).

Built on a knuckle of rock protruding from a boulder-strewn landscape of dramatic dryness, Epano Kastro was constructed by the Venetians in the late 13th century so as to extend their control over the important and fertile interior of the '*Trageia*'—the plain which extends to the east and south of here. All-seeing and always visible, Epano Kastro functioned as a constant reminder of Venetian dominance in an area which was some distance from the island's capital. The site was fortified in prehistoric times and a small stretch of late **Classical walls in isodomic masonry** is visible below the summit. The castle possessed two enceintes: the horse-shoe shaped **barbican** with artillery emplacements (suggesting a later 16th century date) belonged to the outer ring; the curtain-wall higher up was the **inner enceinte**. It was reinforced by three rectangular and three semicircular towers, and enclosed an area with cisterns and living quarters. On the surrounding slopes are several, barrel-vaulted churches—Aghios Giorgios, the Metamorphosis, the Panaghia Kastrianí and the two-aisled catholicon of the Monastery of Aghios Ioannis. The fortress 'seemed by far the most inland spot we had yet visited in the Cyclades,' Theodore Bent commented when he visited in 1883. There remains no trace of the hot springs which he was shown just below the summit, however.

Below Epano Kastro to the southeast, about half way between the castle and Tsikalarió, lies an important and unusual **cemetery of the Geometric period**. (*The tombs are to the south of the footpath to/from Tsikalarió, reached by a path beside a stone wall which runs south and crosses a small, rocky ridge through a defile before descending to the cemetery.*) The cemetery appears to be a collection of monumental family tombs on a plateau. The site is dominated by a **menhir** which stands over 2.5m high. The burial **tumuli**, some of which have a diameter of as much as 12m and were marked by circles of orthostats, are highly unusual for the period. Evidence of the funeral pyres at the centre of the tumuli has been found and a notable quantity of fine wheel-made pottery, painted vessels and jewellery (now in the Naxos Archaeological Museum): this dates mostly from the 9th and 8th centuries BC, and reveals contacts with Attica and other regions of Greece and the Aegean.

In the village of **Tsikalarió** is the church of **Aghios Stefanos** (**D**), with remains of 13th century painting. Uphill, c. 500m to the northeast is the ?7th century basilica church of the Taxiárchis Ráchis at Monikía—a curious, domeless, three-aisled basilica now in ruinous condition, also with vestiges of early paintings.

## Chalkí

After the dry lunar landscape of Epano Kastro, the effect of the olive groves, streams and fruit orchards of the valley around **Chalkí** (17km) is all the more powerful. Chalki was the previous capital of the island until 1925, and is still the centre of the area known as the '*Trageia*' in the last two centuries, and as '*Drymalia*' before that. This is the principal area for the cultivation of olives and of the **Citron tree** (*Citrus medica*), originally valued for its medicinal properties, now used for the production of the island's distinctive liqueur '*Kitron*'. At the heart of the town is one of the island's most important churches for its paintings, the *Protóthronos (**2**), dedicated to the Annunciation of the Virgin. (*Generally closed except for liturgies in the early morning and evening: the pappás, however, is frequently to be seen in the village and will open the church.*)

The exterior of the church does not give away its antiquity, which goes back to its foundation as an Early Christian basilica probably in the 6th century. In the 9th century, the original, three-aisled basilica form was modified by the addition of a central dome and crossing; in the 11th century a vaulted narthex was added to the west, at a slightly skewed angle. For much of its early history the church was the seat of the Orthodox bishop of Naxos—hence its name. In the apse of the sanctuary is a *synthronon* **and marble episcopal throne**. This is flanked by processions of *Apostles* **painted in the 6th or 7th century** which, though damaged by the superimposition of later paintings (now removed), exhibit the characteristic vigour of Early Christian work in their beautifully 'sculpted' robes: in the same campaign of work, the dark-skinned face and intense gaze of *St Isidore of Chios* was painted on the left jamb of the left-hand window above the throne. The *Deësis* in the conch above is painted in a very different visual language: the stylised hair of Christ and the

robe—line-drawn rather than 'sculpted' like those below—
dates from 700 years later (13th century), the last phase
of painting in the church. Some fragments of 9th century,
'aniconic' decoration have also been revealed on the north
crossing vault by the apse. Two other periods of painting are
represented—the finest being the work of a particularly sensitive and graceful painter of the 11th century, who executed
the *Annunciation of the Virgin* and the *Presentation at the
Temple* visible in the south vault below the dome. Beneath
the latter, in less felicitous hand, is the huddled mass of the
*40 Martyrs of Sebaste*, who were condemned to death from
hypothermia in a frozen lake. The dramatic *Christ, ringed
by the Four Archangels and Ten Saints* in the cupola is by yet
another slightly later 11th century hand, who paints with a
noticeably harder edge and less tonal unity of colour, but
with great clarity nonetheless. The paintings in the northwest *parecclesion* (off the narthex) are also probably by this
last artist.

Chalkí and its surrounding villages display a variety of
**domestic architecture**, stretching from the 17th century
Venetian towers to the dignified neoclassical town-houses
of the early 20th century. But above all, it is one of the
richest areas in Greece for its **painted Byzantine rural
churches**. The principal ones here are:

## To the north

*__Aghios Giorgios Diasorítis__ (**3**), *mid-11th century. (Signed on footpath 1km northwest of Chalkí. Generally open 10–2.30 with custodian in summer. Otherwise opening to be arranged with Ephorate.)* Here, by contrast, is a rare example of a church with almost all its painting programme intact, executed all in one campaign, shortly after the building was completed. The work is distinguished by its remarkable chromatic harmony and unity, and by the meditative tranquillity of the style of its master artist. The cycle has recently undergone conservation.

The church—un-plastered and of simple and coherent design—stands in an olive grove on the edge of the village. The interior is clear and spacious for so small a church: the dome is supported on four piers whose surfaces are also decorated. Although the paintings probably all date from a single campaign of painting of the middle of the 11th century, there are at least two hands at work. We see the master in the dignified and beautifully executed figures in the apse—a youthful *Archangel Gabriel* to the left, and an even more youthful and innocent *St George* (centre), flanked by his mother, *St Polychronia*, and his father, *Gerontius*. We recognise the same artist's hand again in the exquisite angels—wings spread—which frame the *Ascension* in the central vault. A quite different soul is at work, however, in the scenes in the upper corners, such as the *Archangel Michael appearing to Joshua* (north east corner, north wall) where a flatness and woodenness reveal a less expert hand. This same artist is at work in the roundels with busts of the saints on the eastern piers. The overall effect of the whole programme is nonetheless moving. No detail is overlooked: even the decoration in the robes of the church fathers in the apse is beautifully echoed in the bands of pure decoration which surround and frame the scenes.

*Church of the* \***Panaghia Damniótissa** (**7**) (*800m northeast of Chalki, west of the road to the Drosianí. Generally open 10–2.30 with custodian in summer. Otherwise opening to be arranged with Ephorate.*) A tiny, free-cruciform, 10th century church with the ruined remains of a (later) narthex to the west. There are chromatically rich paintings in the apse and on other surfaces. Of interest is the particular and idiosyncratic personality of the painter which is revealed in the expressive and stylised modelling of the face, and the laterally elongated eyes. Some finely carved elements from the original templon screen survive, several of which constitute parts of the north window-frame.

*Basilica of* **Aghios Isídoros** (**8**) (*1.5km north of Chalkí, by a track north from a point 600m west of the main junction in the* *village centre. Unlocked.*) An unexpected sight: this is a large 6th or 7th century, ruined basilica with three aisles and a single apse. It has been modified later: its timber roof, being replaced by the existing, stone barrel-vaults in the 10th/11th century, at the same time probably that the flat-roofed narthex was added. The walls are punctuated with *phialosto-mia*—cross-shaped brick decorations (*see below*). No other decoration, apart from fragments of the carved marble parapet of the original church, has survived.

*Double church of the* **Panaghia Theosképasti** *and* **Aghios Spýridon** (**E**) (*by the high school in Chalkí*). Two contiguous single-aisled churches. The conches of the twin apses of the south aisle have 13th century paintings of the *Pantocrator* (north) and the *Virgin 'Nikopoia'* (south).

## At Vourvouriá, south west of Chalkí

**Aghios Konstantínos** (**F**) (*400m outside, and due south, of the village of Vouvouriá, 1km southwest of Chalkí*). Substantial painting remains in the apse of a *Virgin* of the 'Blachernae' type, above beautifully depicted saints below, dated to 1311 by an inscription in the conch.

## At Akadími, east of Chalkí

**Aghios Panteleímon** (**G**) (*500m due south of Chalkí*). 13th century church with contemporaneous paintings, best preserved in the apse and conch, conceived in a highly individualistic style. Note the especially fine *Deësis* with a powerful, central Christ figure.

### At Keramí, east of Chalkí

*Aghios Ioannis Theológos Keramioú* (**9**) (*200m east of the main road passing through Keramí, to the north of the village centre. Open 10–2.30.*) The surviving painting-remains here (recently restored against a rather unsympathetic background colour of plaster) are fragmentary but of high quality, dating from the late 13th century. Because of notable similarities in stylistic traits, it cannot be precluded that the artist is not the same as the artist of Aghios Nikolaos (*see below*), although there is perhaps greater modelling and shading to the faces in the figures here. Behind the real altar, another Holy Table is painted in the apse, covered with a decorated cloth and a paten bearing the words, 'Take, eat: this is my Body'. The church is of the domed-square, 'mausoleum-type'; the vaulted bay to the west and its belfry were added later. The door-frame comprises ancient blocks.

*Aghii Apóstoli* (**10**) (*250 m to the south of the main road passing through Keramí, to the west of the village centre. Locked, but the exterior is of greatest interest.*) An ?11th century church, of interest for its impressive design and sophisticated appearance, set in the midst of olive groves: it has only slight remains of 12th and 13th century paintings within. The building is on an inscribed-cross plan, with a dome supported by free-standing piers. The domed narthex to the west, together with the tall drum of the main dome, creates an exterior profile full of interest. The rising mass of volumes and portals at the west front is particularly striking and is the exterior expression of an architectural anomaly—namely the inclusion of a small, domed oratory on the upper level above the narthex. The south side is beautifully articulated with a blind arcade with 'pendentive' designs between the arches made with *phialostomia*—small, hollow, square or cross-shaped elements in terracotta, which because of their similarity to the crimped mouth of a certain kind of water-jug, are called 'phialo-stomia' ('bottle-mouths'). These were included both for decorative purposes, and to increase ventilation in the walls. They are mostly found on islands such as Chios, with a strong tradition of using brick and tile in buildings, and are unusual here on Naxos.

## The '*pyrgi*'

There are at least four important **fortified manors** or '*pyrgi*' still to be seen in these villages. These structures, though built with a robust four-square design and bearing crenellations and machicolations, were not primarily for defensive purposes but were emblematic of the power and status of the rich families who built them and who controlled their productive lands and serfs from these grand rural homes. The design of all of them is similar in principle: a ground floor given over to vaulted undercrofts for the storage of the produce of their lands, often furnished with cisterns as well; a *piano nobile* above—often accessible by a wooden drawbridge—with a *salone* running the width of the building with rooms off to the side; an upper area for sleeping rooms; and a flat crenellated roof for defence, if necessary, and for the collection of water which was stored in the cisterns below. The **Barozzi-Grazia Tower** in the centre of Chalkí (*northeast of the Portothronos*) was built by Bernardo Barozzi in 1742, though the Eagle of Byzantium and the arms above the door are those of the Frangopoulos family who bought the house in the later part of the same century. The **Markopolitis Tower** in Akadími, and the **Kalavros Tower** in Keramí, built around 1770, both belonged to the Politis family who were prominent in the struggles of the Greek community, first against the Italians, then against the Turks. The oldest '*pyrgos*' in this immediate area is the **Barozzi Tower** in Filoti (20km), built in 1650.

The Barozzi, who married into the Crispi family, owned the majority of the land in this area.

## III. Chora—Galanádo—Sangrí—Apáliros—Aghiasós—Aghios Sozon (30km)

Although different in landscape, this is a route also characterised by a concentration of very fine painted churches and several 17th century towers. The first of these, the **Bellonia Tower**, is on the edge of Galanado (5km southeast of Chora). The 17th century mansion, of impressive dimensions, is now ruined though a number of its marble refinements are still in place. It is thought that it may have been the residence of the Catholic Archbishop of Naxos in the 17th and 18th centuries. Adjacent to it is the **double church of Aghios Giorgios and Aghios Ioannis**. The two barrel-vaulted elements, joined like Siamese twins by two vaulted passages, bear separate dedications. This is an unusual configuration, but one not uncommon in rural Naxos: the parallel sanctuaries may have offered the possibility of accommodating both Orthodox and Roman Catholic congregations under the same roof, suggesting that a satisfactory *modus vivendi* had by this point been established between the two communities in the countryside of Naxos. From Galanado can be visited the churches in the valley of the Parátrechos river to the north: in particular, **Aghios Giorgios Parátrechou** (**H**) (*south of the Galanado to Glinado road*), with 13th century paintings and remains of an earlier church on the site; and **Aghios Nikolaos Parátrechou** (**I**), (*0.5km to the north, by the footpath from the sharp bend before Galanádo*)—an 11th century church of compact and beautifully proportioned architectural form, with antique capitals and marble elements in the interior.

## Around Sangrí

The road continues, through undulating country with good views of the mountains, to the scattered communities of **Kato Sangrí** (10.5km) and **Ano Sangrí** (12km), near to which are two important churches:

*Aghios Artémios* (**11**) (*1.5km east of Kato Sangri; visible in the valley from the Chalkí/Sangri road, c 1.5km north of the Bazaios Tower and 3km south of Chalki. Opening to be arranged with Ephorate.*) An ancient single-aisled domed church of moving simplicity which conserves bands of aniconic decoration in the vault of the sanctuary dating from the 9th century. Some elements of the decoration imitate marble revetment, others have the appearance of decorative ceramic tiles. In the border of the area of spiral volutes is an inscription in red: 'Remember, O Lord, thy servant, Ikonomos, whose name thou knowest. Amen.' It should be noted that everything is hand-drawn, with no stencils or mechanical aids.

***Aghios Nikólaos*** (**12**) (*signed, south from the eastern end of Ano Sangrí: open Mon–Fri 10–2.30 in summer. Otherwise opening to be arranged with Ephorate.*) This has well-preserved areas of painting dating from 1270 in the interior, according to the inscription on the arch of the conch. Striking use is made of azurite and ?cinnebar: in places, finer details have been added *a secco* with a pasty, lead-white. In two of the pendentives of the dome, the Evangelists are represented by a complex motif of *tetramorphs*—the sacred symbols of the Gospel writers. In the middle of the north wall, lower layers of two earlier painting campaigns can be seen, depicting the *Virgin and Child*; the details reveal them to have been of considerable sophistication. Fine scenes of the Baptism—in which a merman symbolizes the River Jordan—and of the *Nativity* decorate the sanctuary vault.

## The churches around the Bazaios Tower

At 12km, the main road turns northeast towards Chalkí; by taking the right fork you come to the **Bazaios Tower** (12.5km), clearly visible ahead at the foot of the mountain. The tower, recently restored, dates from 1671, and functioned, until it was abandoned in the 19th century, as the monastery of the Timios Stavros ('The Venerable Cross'). Four hundred metres south of the Bazaios Tower a track leads off into the fields and skirts the south side of Mount Prophitis Elias. Shortly after passing two concrete cisterns, by the stream bed to the right (1.2km), is the cave chapel of the **Panaghia Spiliótissa** beneath an overhang of rock, occupying the site of an anchorite's hermitage.

The Bazaios Tower is a useful landmark and point of reference for a further selection of important churches in the area. These are:

### Above and to the east

*Monastery of the Nativity, Kalorítissa* (**4**)—*7th–14th centuries. (Partially hidden, but visible, high up on the west slope of the hill of Prophitis Elias above Bazaios Tower; 30-minute climb. Outer area unlocked.)* A cave such as this with a fine panoramic view as far as Paros must have been a place of worship for a long time. The first Christian presence may be of the 4th century: a carved relief of the Nativity of little later than this date (now in the Byzantine Museum in Athens) comes from here. Behind the domed refectory building of the abandoned monastery, which sits on a natural terrace, is a spacious cave out of which has been created the church of the Nativity. Caves—which, since the time of Plato, had signified the benighted status of earthly, human existence—form a marvellous symbolic setting for the Nativity, in which the heavenly Christ takes on earthly humility. The centre of interest is in the apse and conch of the rupestrine church (now unfortunately closed off by a grille): above the *synthronon* and to either side of the episcopal throne are two framed panels of the *Apostles* believed possibly to date from the 7th century, before the Iconoclastic debate. In better condition is the beautiful *Virgin and Child Enthroned* which is framed by two symmetrical deeply bowing figures—John the Baptist and Isaiah: this resonant image dates from the 10th century. The other painting fragments, mostly of later date, include a dramatic *Ascension* in a notably individual style. The monastery was furnished with large, vaulted cisterns whose marble well-heads are visible.

## To the southwest

***Aghios Ioannis Theológos Avlonítsas*** (**J**) (*in the fields southwest of the Bazaios Tower and east of Aghios Nikolaos*). The profile of the church, with high dome and pronounced free-cross plan, is visible form a distance. There are good paintings from the 11th–13th centuries both in the church and in the adjoining chapel of St John the Baptist in the northwest corner.

## To the south

**Panaghia Arkouliótissa** (**K**) (*west of the Chalkí–Aghiasós road, 300m south of Bazaios Tower, opposite the track leading to the Spiliotissa*). A small church of an unmodified inscribed-cross plan, with a handsome, clear-cut profile and high cupola drum. There are remains of high-quality 11th century paintings, and of the carved marble screen.

*****Aghios Ioannis Theológos Adisaroú** (**5**)—*9th century. (In the area of Lathrina, c. 1km east of the site of the Temple of Demeter, in a field 100m to the east of the Chalki/Aghiasos road, 2.5km south of the Bazaios Tower. Opening to be arranged with Ephorate.*) This tiny rural church has been included among the five most important on the island (although opening at the moment (2010) still has to be arranged with the Ephorate) for the reason that it is one of the easiest to find of the few churches on the island decorated with aniconic paintings, dating from the period of the Iconoclastic debate. The rough-stone chapel, with a single vaulted aisle and a low central cupola, is of extreme simplicity and the areas of decoration are patchy but of remarkable beauty. In places—especially in the designs of the sanctuary vault—it is tempting to see patterns similar to contemporary Islamic decoration. But the principal influence is a clear and unbroken memory of Roman *opus sectile* work, best seen in the variety of designs in the conch and apse at the east end. In some small areas even, the colour seems deliberately 'marbled'. Some of the designs look forward to the floors of the Cosmati. The colours—prepared with simple earth pigments, ferric oxides and a pale azurite—are delicate.

***Aghii Giorgios and Nikolaos Lathrínou*** (L) (*100m to the west* of the Chalkí-Aghiasós road, 2.7km south of Bazaios Tower). This is the site of an Early Christian basilica on which two adjoining chapels, dedicated to the two saints, have been built. Some interesting 13th century painting still remains, although the very fine Deësis has now been removed to Athens (Byzantine Museum). The exterior of the west front includes carved, Early Christian marble elements.

## The Archaic Temple of Demeter

A short distance north and west of Lathrina, the **Temple of Demeter** at **Gyroulas** (17.5km) comes into view. The site can equally well be reached directly (15.5km) from Ano Sangrí. The temple has been put immaculately in order in recent times, with substantial elements reconstructed, and a small museum created on the site (*open daily except Mon 8.30–3*). It stands on an eminence surveying an open fertile valley, framed by the mountains to the east and the distant sea to the south. Visible from all around, it must have been felt by the ancient workers on the land as a reassuring and protecting presence. The importance of the archaeological site lies in what it has revealed about the way in which cult and architecture develop together. Sometimes Greek temple-design is thought of as a rigid and repetitive model: this temple shows how flexible and varied it can be. This has been made particularly clear by the good archaeological display.

Cult on this hill goes back at least to the 8th century BC, when deities of the fertility of the land were propitiated in the open air in the area under, and in front of, the existing temple. The excavations have revealed interconnected **shallow cultic pits** in this area for the offering of the produce of the land to the deities. Around 530 BC, during the period of the rule of Lygdamis and of the building of the Portara, a temple was erected here which had the plan of a '*thesmophoreion*', i.e a place of cult of the chthonic divinities of the land and its fertility: this is the **Temple of Demeter** whose remains are most visible today. It was constructed entirely in marble: even the beams and tiles which comprised the roof were of local stone. This was a courageous innovation, involving newly developed technologies; but it had been attempted before by the Naxiots, most notably in their *Oikos* in the Sanctuary of Apollo on Delos. The temple was also ground-breaking in other aspects of design. It had a south facing portico or *pronaos*, with five columns *in antis*. Two large framed doorways led from this porch into the enclosed interior whose pitched marble roof was supported by a transverse row of columns whose heights varied with the slopes of the roof.

To the west side of the site a magnificent example of one of the **marble beams** of the *pronaos* is preserved. Beams such as this supported the horizontal coffered ceiling which covered the pronaos. The interior of the building, by contrast, had no flat ceiling below its pitched roof. This gave rise to an elating sensation of increased height and space as you passed from the porch to the interior of the temple. The roof-tiles were made in a marble chosen for its translucence, which must have transmitted a beautiful, subdued luminousness into the interior on sunny days.

With the arrival of Christianity, the temple was converted into a church: this happened in two phases and involved reconfiguring the building to accommodate the different orientation required by a Christian place of worship. The portico to the south was filled up between the columns to create a lateral narthex. A doorway was made in the west wall; then in the 6th century an apse was created to the east.

The small **museum** below the temple to the west displays the decorative architectural elements and the smaller finds from the site in two rooms, reflecting the two periods of the building's history—Ancient and Early Christian. These include architectural elements, such as the marble tiles of the ancient temple and the carved templon screen of the church, and a small display of the votive offerings found.

## Apaliros Castle

Looking from the Temple of Demeter, the southeast horizon is dominated by the oldest of the surviving mediaeval fortresses on Naxos, **Apaliros Castle** (475 m a.s.l.). (*A track leading east from a point 2km south of the Bazaios Tower—just beyond the turn, west, for the Temple of Demeter—passes over a torrent bed, through a settlement and ends: a 45 minute climb southeast from where the main track ends, brings you to the castle.*) More than a point of surveillance and defence, this was a refuge to which the local population and their livestock could retreat in times of threat. The enceinte is large (c. 300m x 80m), and the remains of cisterns, houses and churches, suggest that there was a permanent living community here.

There were probably prehistoric fortifications on this site, but the castle itself was begun in the 8th century, as a vital protection against the first Arab raids. It became the main stronghold of Byzantine Naxos. The sea is visible, but the site itself is a sufficiently protected distance from it; it dominated the main areas of agricultural production in the south of the island and was quickly accessible from them. When Marco Sanudo came to Naxos in 1207, he landed to the south of here, burned his ships and took five weeks to capture this stronghold from a group of Genoese freebooters who were holding it. Afterwards he built his own castle in Chora and left this one unaltered, so that it remains in form and design substantially an Early Byzantine fortress. The **walls** and the fine **semi-circular bastion** have remained in good condition at the north west corner—the castle's most vulnerable point. There has survived a remarkable number of **vaulted cisterns** (more than 30), amongst the ruins of the houses in the interior. Towards the eastern edge are the remains of the 8th century, church of **Aghios Giorgios**, with two aisles and apses, and a second church added to its south side.

In a remote and beautiful valley, 2km as the crow flies to the east of the castle is the church of **Aghios Giorgios** at **Upper Marathós** (**M**), with 13th century paintings and unusual architectural design. (*3.5km south of Bazaios Tower, a track leads east towards the south side of Apaliros Castle, ending after 2km below the southwestern ascent to the castle; a path for a further 3km skirts south, round the hill and climbs the valley eastwards up to Aghios Giorgios. Allow 3 hours, return*). This is a fine and idiosyncratic church in a wild and dramatic mountain setting. It comprises a main domed aisle (with unusual intersecting vaults creating groin-ribs in the dome), an adjoining barrel-vaulted chapel to the south, and a domed narthex to the west. The church's late 13th century paintings of considerable accomplishment are preserved, amongst which are figures of patrons.

## Aghiasós

South of Lathrina and of Apaliros Castle, the valley is flat and opens out to east and west; it is run through by seasonal torrents, the vegetation is sparse and interspersed with outcrops of rock. From Aghiasós (24km), two 13th century painted churches can be visited in the low hills to the east: the **Panaghia at Archáto (N)**, reached by backtracking 4km to the northeast—a church of curious form which has developed by additions over time, and which conserves paintings, dated to 1285 from an inscription with the names of artist and patrons; and the remarkable church of the **Panaghia Galloús (13)** which lies substantially inland from the shore to the south, at 4.5km from Aghiasós. This is a small, rural, 'mausoleum-type' church. What is interesting here is the quite distinct personality of the artist, who was working in the penultimate decade of the 13th century. One of the several clearly visible inscriptions (which are all votive entreaties of individuals, or of husbands and wives) is dated with the year 6796 since creation, i.e. 1288/89. The artist's colours are rich and the faces he depicts are sensitive and subdued, yet with a graceful and quite idiosyncratic elongation. The faces of the *Baptist* in the conch and of *Christ* on the south wall are particularly worthy of note: they are without any rigidity. The church was originally a small, domed square: the extension to the west is of later date.

The coastal track south along the coast to the tip of the island, ends at the tiny Byzantine church of **Aghios Sozon Kalantou** (30km), built into the rocks in gratitude for the safe rescue of sailors from a shipwreck.

## IV. Chora—Yria—Pláka—Mikrí Vígla—Pyrgáki (20km)

From the southeast corner of the ring-road of Chora, a road heads south for Aghia Anna and the island's (currently) tiny airport. After less than 1km a left branch leads to the **Sanctuary of Dionysos at Yria** (3.8km). (*Open daily except Mon 8.30–3.*) The island of Naxos was sacred to Dionysos, and this spot in the well-watered plain of the Parátrechos river was his main place of cult from at least the 8th century BC. There are many similarities between the final temple built here and the temple of Demeter at Gyroulas (see above)—in their design, orientation (to south), and their evolution and growth from previous places of cult: but there are many significant differences, and the sanctuary here was both older and grander. At its zenith in the 6th century BC, it consisted of a walled rectangular precinct (c. 100m x 50m), with a marble temple, an altar, a *propylon*, several *hestiatoria* and other ancillary buildings.

The site developed through four principal phases.

- Through the 9th and 8th centuries BC, there would have been a small mud-brick shrine with a flat roof and door on the site, and a central sacrificial pit, built over the site of a Mycenaean open-air shrine of considerable antiquity.

- Around 730 BC this was refashioned, in larger size (c. 11 x 16.5 m), with stone walls and wooden posts on marble bases in the interior, which supported a wooden ceiling.

- 50 years later (680 BC) this was modified again and now began to acquire the appearance of a temple with the addition of a four-columned porch on the front. A more uncluttered interior was created with only two rows of wooden columns to support the flat roof which flanked the central focus of the sacrificial pit. This building stood for a century.

- Around 580 BC the first all-stone temple, whose remains are visible today, was constructed on the same site, but with substantially larger proportions (28.4 x 14m). The walls were of granite but the roof tiles, the south wall and the four-column porch were built in contrasting white marble. The interior columns (c. 8m high) were also in marble; they framed the central view towards a large, chryselephantine statue of Dionysos in the rear chamber.

The Ionic capitals surmounting the columns were fully developed in design and very finely cut—although lacking something of the marvellous plasticity of the early Ionic capitals at the Heraion on Samos. A representative example is exhibited here on the top of a concrete stand. To the west of the temple is a marble well-shaft, and the base of a *propylon* which would have formed a monumental entrance into the sanctuary from the city. It is possible that the gigantic, Archaic statue of Dionysos, lying unfinished in its quarry at Apollonas at the northern tip of the island, was intended for this sanctuary.

## ON THE PRESENTATION OF ARCHAEOLOGICAL
### SITES

In the heyday of Romantic archaeology, when Heinrich Schliemann, Arthur Evans and Theodore Bent came to the Greek islands, the sites they visited were mostly untouched—overgrown with vegetation, pastured by animals, and subject to the degradation of time and weather. Today the same sites are a vulnerable prey to the expansion of urban areas, road networks and of the pressures of more intensive farming and rural building. There are many more sites known now, and there is a much greater public interest in seeing them. How is it possible to reconcile respect for the nature of a ruin with its proper protection? How can presenting archaeological material coherently to the public be reconciled with leaving a ruin as what it is—namely a ruin; something whose appeal lies in the fact that it is in the open and not in the closed context of a museum display case; i.e. something that has, above all, a character and atmosphere?

A lot of funding, thought and effort has been spent in particular on Naxos for the presentation of archaeological areas to the public. There have been some extraordinary successes—and a few less successful endeavours. The covered excavations in Mitropoleos Square in Naxos stand as a model of the very best museological presentation of archaeological finds, in which a complex history is clearly and concisely displayed and explained: the visitor is given a privileged glimpse into a fascinating discovery, and helped to share both the sense of discovery as well as the often difficult decisions that archaeologists face as they pick their way through a tissue of superimposed, equally valid layers of history. Furthermore, the excavations and their protective covering have had the least possible aesthetic impact on the living environment at the heart of the modern town. A notable success, in short.

Unlike underground excavations, the Temple of Dionysos at Yria was a rural site of considerable personality. Its current presentation is an example of how easily over-management can kill the spirit of such a place. Once a place of profound cultic importance, today it has been reduced to a document. What is called 'enhancement'—the fencing, the gravel paths and corrals, the inappropriate municipal vegetation, and above all the heavy-handed reorganisation with new, machine-cut marble slabs and concrete plinths—in the end alienates, rather than enhances. It becomes intrusive in a place of cult and of ruined antiquity. The archaeologists have painstakingly revealed a site of immense importance; but officialdom has rendered it almost perfectly sterile.

Notwithstanding, on 4 June 2003, in the presence of the Prince Consort of Denmark, President of *Europa Nostra*, and high officials of the European Union, the Category 1D Award for 'outstanding heritage achievements' was given for the sanctuaries of Dionysos at Yria and of Demeter at Sangrí, in recognition of their presentation and reconstruction. The future will probably see many more ruined, rural sanctuaries turned in this manner into extensions of the urban context.

To the west of Yria lie the flat salt-marshes of the Parátrechos stream, bordered to the west by the rocky outcrop of **Aghios Prokópios**, and by the long sandy **beaches of Aghios Giorgios**, to north, and **Aghia Anna**, to south. Due south of Yria, and accessible from the road from Vivlos to Plaka (on a hillside to the north, 1.5km west of Vivlos) is the **Hellenistic tower of Plaka** (8.5km). The building is about 11m square and of equivalent height, constructed in an immaculate isodomic granite masonry which suggests a date of the late 4th century BC. Its position would appear to preclude its having been a watch-tower: the site of the windmills above would have been more appropriate for that. It must represent a fortified rural building whose purpose was to survey and protect the productive valley of Plaka below. Just across the road in the valley lies the church of **Aghios Matthaios**, built on the site of an Early Christian basilica, from which some vestiges of mosaic floor, architectural fragments and a baptismal font survive on site. Three kilometres south of Vivlos (formerly called 'Tripodes') is the church of **Aghios Ioannis Theológos Kaknádou** (**O**), with 13th century paintings of distinctive style and chromatic range.

The long, sweeping bays of the west coast are interrupted by the rocky knob of **Mikrí Vígla** (17.5km), which projects into the sea at one of the most exposed points on the coast, between two shallow coves. Excavations on and around the summit of the outcrop have revealed a stone construction of the Middle Bronze Age where clay figurines, pottery (of Minoan influence) and fragments of wall-paintings have been unearthed. Mikri Vigla, which appears to have flourished in the early 2nd millennium

BC at a time when other Early Cycladic settlements were being abandoned, represents an important piece in the jigsaw of a wider understanding of the prehistoric Cyclades. In spite of its healthy survival into the Middle Bronze Age, it too succumbed shortly after 1500 BC to the growing concentration and centralisation of settlement at Grotta (modern Chora), which left the other island centres largely empty.

Visible to the east of the main road, shortly after the turning for Mikri Vigla is a 17th century '*pyrgos*', known as the **Oskelos Tower**, now abandoned except for a large community of doves. Above it on the hill is the church of **Aghios Giorgios Oskelou (P)**, and to its north the church of **Aghios Ioannis Oskelou**. Both preserve interesting late 13th century paintings, and the former incorporates large blocks of antique marble and carved Early Byzantine pieces. There are several natural outcrops of fine marble in the area.

The landlocked salt-pools, reed-beds and marshes which lie behind the stretches of sand on this coastline constitute a stopping-point on the migration route of a magnificent variety and quantity of birds in the spring: these include the collared flycatcher, the rare (in Europe) Isabelline wheatear, red-throated pipits, shrikes and red-footed falcon. At the southwest corner of the island, below Kastraki (17km) the dunes are densely covered in juniper, dwarf-cedar and arbutus, with sea-thyme on the surface. To the east of the point stretches the sheltered **bay of Pyrgaki** (20km) with beautiful sands.

# NORTHERN NAXOS

Apart from the alluvial plain of Engares, the northwest coast of Naxos is wild, rocky and mostly deserted: the twisting road that rounds the northern tip of the island and finishes at Apollonas is of recent completion. These were the lands of the Venetian, Cocco family whose two impressive towers punctuate the coastline.

Two kilometres out of Chora to the north, after passing the turns for the fortified, 18th century monastery of Aghios Ioannis Chrysostomos on the hillside to the right-hand side, the road makes a sharp turn around a creek. Above the bend can be seen the whitewashed chapel of **Aghios Ioannis Pródromos** (*unlocked*). The interior has small areas of 15th century painting in the apse; the beautiful and expressive face of *Christ on the Cross* in the niche of the apse, and the saint to the right, are of particular note. Directly below—but now almost completely

obscured by oleander bushes—stands what is left of the
**fountain-house of Ismail Hasan Ağa**, built in 1759 by
the Ottoman governor of Naxos. This is the last remaining, substantial Ottoman monument on the island.

After 4km, a track leads off to the left, and winds into
an area of hilly scrub, dropping eventually to the **Ypsili
Tower**, the largest of the fortified manor/monasteries on
the island, built at the beginning of the 17th century by
the Cocco family. The tower, though somewhat hidden,
dominates the fertile Engares valley. After a further 2km
along the main road beyond the turning for Ypsili, by taking the road left for Galini and continuing through the village towards the beach, you come (on the right) to the 9th
century church of the **Koimisis tis Theotokou** or '**Panaghia Attaliótissa**' (**Q**), sited at the edge of a sea of green-
ery. This is a beautifully proportioned building with a
cross-in-square plan, forming three aisles and apses. Some
14th century painting of considerable sophistication survives, as well as fragments of a carved marble throne or
ambo from the original foundation on the site. To the left
of the entrance gate, a frieze with triglyphs is built into
the perimeter wall, along with other spolia taken from an
ancient building in the valley—possibly the Temple of
Athena *Poliouchos*, which is believed to have stood in the
valley a short distance to the north of **Engarés** (7.5km).

After these fertile fields between Galini and Engarés which grow fruit and vegetables for the city, the coastline becomes steeper, more barren and much less populated. As the road comes to a water reservoir at 15km, a track heads into the steep interior of the Koronos massif, with its peak at Mavro Vouni, ('Black Mountain'—997m). The track leads to the villages of Skepóni and Myrísis, after three and six kilometres climb respectively. On the hillside south of **Skepóni** is the ruined church of **Aghios Giorgios (R)**, with remains of 13th and 14th century layers of painting. Remote and scenic **Myrísis** is a good centre for walks which explore the valleys of the north of the island; the route from Myrísis to Koronída (Komiáki) is particularly rewarding.

Before the northern tip of the island, the road passes (24km) above a bay where the whitewashed, 9th/10th century church of **Aghios Theodoros (S)**, built on the site of an Early Christian predecessor, is visible just behind the shore. Not far beyond, the striking profile and position of the crenellated **Tower of Aghiá** (27.5km), built in 1717, comes into view, impressively sited at a height of over 200m above the shore of the northern tip of the island. This is the second of the towers built on this coast by the Cocco family. The interior is derelict and the floors have collapsed, leaving fireplaces suspended at the upper levels. Entrance was originally by a wooden ladder: the stairs to the door were probably added in the last century. The holes for the fixing of scaffolding during construction are still visible in the walls. A stepped path to the east leads down to the spring and to the picturesque setting of the **monastery of Aghiá (T)**, founded in the 12th century and rebuilt in the 17th century at the time the tower was erected.

The road rounds the northern tip of the island and finally drops down to sea-level, regaining human habitation at the village of **Apóllonas** (35km), set between two small coves on the northeastern tip of the island. The gigantic *\***abandoned *kouros* of Apollonas lies in the cradle of its own quarry, just above and to the west of the main road, 500m south of the harbour. This massive figure, 10.7m in stature and probably representing the bearded god Dionysos, would, if it had been completed, have been the largest solid monolithic sculpted figure of Classical Antiquity. Its dimensions and boldness still astonish.

Because they are unfinished and considerably eroded, it is notoriously difficult to date these pieces, but the work is believed to have been begun around 550 BC, slightly later than the estimated date for the Flerio *kouroi*. Larger tools have been used here than at Flerio: the upper surface is covered with the marks of a very large bronze point, used once again perpendicularly to the surface. Around the supine figure, the native rock bears the parallel striations left from the 'cleaning' of the surface, after the stone had been cored out with drills and picks in order to free and delineate the statue. A perfectly cylindrical hole in the rock scarp beside the feet of the statue served as a capstan-hole for the winching of debris out from the long, narrow space. The projecting arms and hands—a position for receiving offerings—have broken and eroded with time, but the eyes, nose, beard and pectorals all retain some definition.

It is possible that the figure was destined for the sanctuary of Dionysos at Yria. Once again this presents considerable difficulties of transportation—here more than ever, given an estimated weight of 130 tons. The descent to the sea is steep: the beginnings of the stone ramp which had to be cut down to the shore is just visible to the right of the steps as you climb up.

Above Apollonas on the sharp summit (355m) to the southeast of the village, are the remains of the most inaccessible of the island's Venetian fortresses, **Kalogeros Castle** which surveys the open waters and sea passages of the Icarian Sea. Once again the fortress (*accessible by path from the main road, above a hair-pin bend 5km south* *of Apollonas, at the turning for Mesi*) is built on the site of earlier Byzantine and prehistoric fortifications.


# APEIRANTHOS AND EASTERN NAXOS


**Apeíranthos** (25.5km from the port) is a very different world from Chora, and even from the Trageia below it. High up, steep and often cloud-strafed, the forbidding settlement of marble houses and marble streets is cut off from the rest of the island by the sharp central ridge of mountains which runs at a height of 750–850m directly behind the village. The Naxiots believe the village was originally settled by Cretans in the 10th century. Theodeore Bent commented that 'everywhere on Naxos they have a bad word for the people of Apeiranthos; a village of robbers… away in the mountains'. Because of its remoteness (until the asphalt road was built), it has always been an independent and naturally conservative community: this has meant that it has preserved traditions of song and dance and versifying which other communities have lost, and which still emerge at celebratory occasions such as baptisms and weddings.

Apeíranthos remains the principal point of reference

for the unpopulated eastern half of the island, and the roads to the north, northeast and southeast corners of the island all pass through it. Because it clings to a marble scarp, the village has no natural centre but spreads to either side of a winding central street paved in marble. The thoroughfare begins beside the finely carved gateposts of the broad-set, 18th century church of the **Panaghia Apeiranthítissa**, and curves round the hill, passing terraces of prosperous houses, sometimes set back behind a solid 'fence' or balcony of white marble panels and posts—a feature unique to Apeiranthos. The street opens sufficiently to accommodate a tiny shaded *plateia* partly tucked beneath a section of the natural rock scarp which weeps water onto the marble steps below. From above, the two 17th century '*Pyrgi*' **of the Zevgoli and Bardanis** families dominate the village.

Of the four small museums—the **Geology Museum**, **Natural History Museum** (palaeontology, fossils and marine specimens), **Folklore Museum** (textiles, embroideries and domestic objects) and the **Archaeology Museum**—the last should not be missed, even though its opening times can be hard to predict. (*Open summer only 9–3, closed Mon*) It exhibits Cycladic artefacts from the 3rd millennium BC—bowls, 'chalices', figurines and clay pieces, among which is a burnished and perforated clay cup with a handle which has been dubbed an 'incense-burner'. The collection's most remarkable treasures are the rough-hewn limestone slabs whose smoothest faces have been decorated with ***pecked and chipped designs** showing the life of early Bronze Age man: human figures husbanding horned animals, men apparently standing in a boat, etc. These come from the excavations of what may have been an open-air shrine on the island's east coast, south of Kanáki, at Korfi tou Aroniou; they are dated to the late 3rd millennium BC.

The area immediately around Apeiranthos has a number of fine early Byzantine churches. The most nota-ble is **Aghia Kyriakí Kalonís (14)**, which has an array of rare, 9th century aniconic wall-paintings. The church lies camouflaged (though not out of sight) against the stony hillside in the deep valley to the northeast of the village. (*A foot-path, c. 4.5km, descends from the main road almost opposite the small 'Natural History Museum', and takes at least one hour each way. Unlocked.*)

This is the last and perhaps most unusual of the group of churches with aniconic decorations of the 9th century. Al-though only fragmentary, they nonetheless reward the long walk here. The designs are of greatest interest in the lower apse where a dozen fantastic birds (?roosters)—perhaps symbolising the Apostles who would normally be figured here—as well as palm trees and fish, fill the space. The birds have plumes and strange knobs on their joints, and are more gracefully depicted on the right, than on the left—as if by two different hands. The remainder of the decoration which patchily covers the surfaces of the sanctuary is predominantly patterned or marbled. The church is constructed in dry masonry and floored with large flagstones; the megalithic posts and lintel of the west door from the narthex, enhance the overall impression of entering an ancient tomb, which is only alleviated by the luminous cupola. It is probable that the whole ensemble of the church—the main aisle and sanctuary, the subsidiary aisle to the south, and the narthex—was conceived as a unified design.

In the cultivated valley to the south of Apeiranthos (east of the main road) are the adjacent, painted churches of **Aghios Pachomios** and **Aghios Giorgios (U)**. (*On arriving in Apeiranthos from the south, take the concrete road to right immediately on entering habitation.*) The smaller church, Aghios Giorgios, dating from the ?11th century, is now in poor condition and has only vestiges of painting (dated 1254 from the inscription); the masonry templon screen in the interior is—unusually—a structural element partially supporting the dome here. Aghios Pachomios, of the 13th century, conserves fine paintings, however. The *Transfiguration* (south), *Crucifixion* (north), *Archangel Michael*, and *St John* (northwest pendentive) are noteworthy, as are the full-length Angels of the dome. Further east from the two churches, built against an overhang in the rock are the ruins of **Aghios Ermolaos** with traces of an-iconic decoration (mainly geometric patterns) in the vault.

## NORTH OF APEIRANTHOS

The tortuous and panoramic road north towards Apollonas, reaches an exposed watershed at Stavrós (31km), with magnificent *views to west (Paros) and east (Donousa). Branch roads lead west to the villages of **Keramotí**—set on a spur in a deep declivity, hidden from sight—and the deserted settlement of **Síphones**, above which is the double church of **Aghios Ioannis and Aghios Giorgios (V)** (*visible below the road to the west before reaching Siphonés*). This is a complex of two 11th century, intercommunicating churches, one of which (north) is domed and given greater architectural importance by the presence of a *synthronon* and throne. Both have fragments of 13th/14th century painting conserving strong colour; there are vigorous figures of an *Archangel* and a

*Hierarch* to either side of the conch in the north church. Beyond Siphones, the road continues to Moní, the Drosianí church, and eventually to Chalkí after 11.5km.

Just before the next village of Kóonos, two roads branch to the east within 500m of one another. The first branch (at 33km: signed 'Panaghia Argokiliótissa') leads down to Atsipápi a mediaeval settlement with fine dry-stone terraces, now mostly abandoned. The road passes the pilgrimage place of the miraculous icon of the **Panaghia Argokiliótissa** ('slow dripping'), which was found in a cave here with a weak, dripping spring of 'holy' water, or *aghiasma*. The original 18th century church is of a curiously long low rectangular form, designed to accommodate crowds on pilgrimage days: its length is nicely punctuated by a broad belfry half way along. A modern church of much larger dimensions is under construction just above.

The second branch east from the main road (at 33.5km: signed 'Lionas') leads into the heart of the **emery mining area**, and ends at the small coastal settlement of **Liónas**, 8km below, which still survives with a couple of tavernas even though the mines are now virtually closed. The road descends through a steep and arid landscape, transformed by the human quest for this mineral which has been pursued here for several millennia. Emery was the most valuable and unique of the island's exports, and until the development of synthetic abrasives in the last century, Naxos alone supplied it to the Western world's markets throughout the centuries. The material, in impure form, can still be collected on the surface. The industrial method of extracting surface deposits by the process of 'fire-setting' is described below, and it is this which has contributed more to the deforestation of this area of the island than anything else. To the right of the road, galleries can be seen perforating the mountainside—the rails, for transporting the material from the mine-face, still projecting beyond the entrances. Half way down the ravine a road to the left cuts back down to the principal loading station and sorting centre. The blocks were cleaned of extraneous impurities here, loaded into overhead gondolas and transported over the ridge to the south and down to the boat-loading station in the port of Moutsoúna. The line of the overhead cables can still be followed on its 9km journey. The mines were producing an average of 10,000 tons of emery per year prior to the Second World War.

## MARBLE AND EMERY

A pure white marble, of extremely fine quality, and a hard rock known as 'black sand' or emery, have together constituted the economy and the influence of Naxos throughout most of its history. Their importance is hard to overestimate: the foundations of marble sculpting for Western art were laid in Naxos, because of the quality of its primary material, and up until the last century, the island was the only major source of emery in the Western world for more than 3,000 years. The two materials first visibly come together in the world of the Early Cycladic sculptures of the 3rd millennium BC: the white translucent marble was sympathetic to the elegantly simple forms of the figurines and cups, and the softness of their contours could only have been achieved by painstaking working and polishing with the emery and pumice. The materials suggested the style; and the figures enhanced the materials.

Naxos marble is a prince among marbles: it is worth picking some up, handling it, and examining it in the light. Its regular crystalline structure is so open that it is almost translucent. That is why the an-

cient builders were able to roof the Temple of Demeter at Sangrí with marble tiles and still be sure that
the interior would be suffused with a gentle light. It is
acknowledged among sculptors that the world's most
suitable marbles for sculpture are those from Paros
and Naxos. Michelangelo and Bernini would have
used them, if they had been more readily available to
them. The Carrara marble which they used instead
(and which the Romans called *marmor lunensis*) is
perhaps purer, but it is quite different in character. Its
colour is colder and bluer, and it is of a more regular
and compact structure, imparting a 'sugary' quality to
the stone: it is harder and less responsive to the chisel
than Naxos or Paros marble, and it lacks their warmth
and translucence. Nor do its crystals glint in such a
lively fashion. Naxos was able to lead the Greek world
in marble sculpting in the 6th century BC, because it
had the best primary material, and as a consequence
it produced, both for itself and for Delos, the greatest marble statuary of the age. Its hegemony was not
to last for long, however: in the next century, Paros
and Athens, both with enviable qualities of marble of
their own, challenged her supremacy.

Emery is marble's alter ego: much harder and stronger, and dark grey to black in colour. It is composed principally of corundum (aluminum oxide), mixed with small proportions of iron ore and magnetite. It abrades any softer stone, such as marble, without leaving scores or traces of colour, and can polish surfaces to considerable softness, especially when combined with volcanic pumice. It was also used as an abrasive for sharpening metal tools and weapons. In earliest times it was obtained, in the eastern valleys of Naxos, from loose rocks and boulders which had been exposed to weathering; but during the Ottoman occupation it was first deep-mined and extracted from the mountainsides. The ancient Greeks called emery, 'σμύρις'. From Naxos the mineral was shipped to Smyrna (Izmir) in the eastern Aegean, where its principal market and distribution-centre was. It is not improbable, therefore, that the name 'Smyrna' comes from 'smyris'. The Romans called emery 'naxium'. Its qualities and uses are mentioned by Theophrastus, Dioscorides and Pliny. Until 20th century mining techniques were introduced, the surface emery deposits were detached by 'fire-setting', i.e. heating a prepared area for several hours by the burning of a fire on the surface; the subsequent dousing of the heated area with cold water, caused the rock to fracture along its natural faults, facilitating its breaking up and extraction.

Abrading or 'polishing' with emery was the last phase in the working of a marble artefact. In the discussion of the unfinished *kouroi* (above), mention has been made of the tools and working practices of the early sculptors. It must be remembered that although iron was known and used in the 7th and 6th centuries BC, it was still a precious metal and remained the preserve of the rich and the warrior-classes, principally for weaponry. Sculptors still had to make do with softer tools of bronze. This is why the surface of a marble block that was going to be sculpted had to be beaten and 'bruised' first of all, before it was cut. This ruptured the crystalline structure of the stone and made it much more sensitive to the strokes of the bronze tools. When a sculpture was completed, however, the crystalline structure was once again altered, this time by the abrading with emery. This slowly compacted the fractured crystals in the surface so that they began to reflect light, i.e. to shine or acquire a 'polish'. At the same time, by compressing the surface, the abrasion created a kind of protective 'skin' for the marble, which impeded the absorption of corrosive elements into the heart of the stone which might cause it to decay and erode. This is what conservators, such as those working on the Parthenon, are referring to when they say that (modern industrial) pollution has eaten through the 'skin of the marble' laying it wide open to a corrosion in the interior of the blocks, which leads eventually to its crumbling. The sections of the Parthenon's frieze exhibited in Athens, show this all too clearly—both the areas where the surface 'skin' has held up and preserved the refined detail of the carving, as well as where it has been eroded and has turned to little more than illegible, powdered gypsum.

The domestic architecture of Apeiranthos and the other villages along the island's northern ridge of mountains—**Keramotí**, **Kóronos**, **Skadó**, **Koronída** (named from the nymph, *Koronis*, who reared Dionysos in a cave here, and often called by its older name, 'Komiaki') and **Mési**—re-

veal a prosperity which has been underpinned historically by two things: emery mining and agriculture—in particular the production of an excellent wine. A number of
the valleys between them are meticulously stepped with
banks of dry-stone terraces, growing vines. What the olive tree is to the *Trageia*, the vine—and its patron divinity,
Dionysos—is to this area. The springs, threshing floors,
water mills for grain, olive-presses, wine-presses, and the
terraces without number, all form a well-preserved and
self-sufficient agricultural unity on this 'roof' of the island.

## EAST AND SOUTHEAST OF APEIRANTHOS: MOUTSOUNA TO PANORMOS

(*This is an excursion of 28km each way, from Apeiranthos
down to the deserted southeastern extremity of the island,
with only the same road to return by. There are no petrol
facilities on the route.*)

For the last 5km of the descent through the hills to the
coast at Moutsoúna, the overhead cable-way which comes
from the emery mines at Stravolangáda and crosses the
ridge, can be seen to the north. This ambitious project
was necessary because the only harbour deep enough

to receive cargo ships for loading the emery blocks was **Moutsoúna** (36.5km from Chora). Some of the buildings of the loading station can still be seen by the shore. Moutsoúna is a tranquil fishing harbour nowadays, with two good fish tavernas, and an attractive beach at Azalá, 1.5km to its north.

In the foothills to the interior of the coast there are many isolated Byzantine churches, most of them in a state of ruin. Just visible from the road at Ligaridia, 2km south of Moutsouna, is the unusual, flat-roofed church of **Prophitis Elias Vlacháki** (**W**) with 13th century paintings inside. (*A track leads west, inland for 1.5km, from which a footpath climbs up to the south: access difficult.*) The church appears to be built on the site of a prehistoric fort. This is not an uncommon occurrence on this eastern seaboard of Naxos, which was populated with settlements in prehistoric times, and has proven to be archaeologically rich. The limestone slabs with prehistoric, 'pecked' reliefs dating from the 3rd millennium BC, exhibited in the museum of Apeiranthos, come from a panoramic site, by Kleidós Bay (48.5km), known as Korfí tou Aroníou, about half way between Kanáki and Panormos. The most dramatic and beautiful of all Naxos's prehistoric sites, however, is above the sheltered bay of **Pánormos** (54km). At this point, Koufonisi and the other islands to the south seem so close across the generally calm sound of water that this settlement feels no longer a part of Naxos, but part of the wider community of these islands instead. The hill to the west of the bay forms a natural acropolis: on its crown, an Early Cycladic citadel of the 3rd millennium BC has been excavated. The **paved entrance** (running due east/west) flanked by stone 'benches' to either side, leading to a gateway made of larger blocks, is well-preserved and clearly visible, while inside is a tight-knit web of building foundations and alley-ways. The defensive walls here may have been added after the founding of the settlement, in the face of dangers perceived by the inhabitants at the end of the Early Bronze Age. The higher hill, a little way to the north, is crowned with what appear to be Byzantine fortifications, which are built in part over ancient walls. This was an important surveillance point in all periods: today it is a place of great beauty and tranquillity.

## SOUTH OF APEIRANTHOS

Four kilometres south of Apeiranthos, just before the main road to Chora begins to descend to Filoti, a sharp turning to the east climbs over the ridge to Danakós and the *monastery of Christós Fotodóti** (15), 'giver of light', (*left branch after 1km*) the best preserved of the island's '*pyrgi*' monasteries, although in this case the monastery and church existed long before they were 'encased' in a *pyrgos* in the 16th century. The approach to the panoramic site, high on an open mountainside overlooking the east coast, is through an area scattered with magnificent oak trees.

The church here became a dependency of the monastery of St John on Patmos in the 16th century, which may explain the similarity of appearance—a square, castellated, tower with massive buttresses at several points. Its origins however go back to Early Christian times. The *synthronon* and walls of the three-aisled, original basilica have been preserved, although the design was radically altered in the 16th century to turn the church into a square inscribed-cross plan, with dome supported on columns and a narthex to the west. The interior gives a sense of space and unexpected lightness. The building of the high walls of the fortress all round in the 16th century, permitted the creation of an upper level for a refectory and cells, through which the cupola of the *catholicon* now protrudes somewhat oddly.

At the cemetery of the village of **Danakós** (26km from Chora, via Filoti), which lies in a ravine with watermills, is the 9th century church of **Aghios Ioannis Theologos**

(**X**): it preserves a dedicatory inscription, and vestiges of
an-iconic decoration in the north side of the apse.

## MOUNT ZAS AND ZAS CAVE

The road for the **Cave of Zas** branches west 1km after
Filoti (20km), as you head towards Apeiranthos. It finishes after 1.3km at the plentiful springs of sweet water at Ariés which rise in a break of plane-trees offering
stunning views as far as the sea to the southwest, along
a gorge scattered with oak, cypress and olive trees. From
the spring it is a 25-minute steep climb up a torrent bed
to the cave which lies to the left just above another, weak
spring. The combination of nearby fresh-water and protection which the cave affords has appealed since earliest
times, when Neolithic man both dwelled and buried his
dead within this cave. The remarkable finds from this
period in the cave have included clay seal-impressions,
which may suggest the evolving need to identify property which was personal to one family or group. Copper tools were also uncovered. But the most dramatic
find here has been a small beaten gold strip (now in the
Naxos Archaeology Museum, *see above*), dating from the
5th/4th millennium BC, which indicates probable trade
communication with the Northern Aegean and Mac-

edonia. The piece is perforated at its four corners, as if for stringing as an item of jewellery. Throughout the Bronze Age the cave continued to be used; the low transverse wall inside the entrance to the cave dates from this period.

From the cave, the **summit of Zas** (999m) can be reached in a further 45 minutes. This approach is particularly steep. The longer approach from the north, leaving from the road to Danakós, close by the church of Aghia Marina, is more gradual (90 minutes). Zas is the highest peak of the Cyclades, sacred to Zeus, with whom its name is cognate. This is the best area for glimpsing the colony of **Griffon vultures** which inhabit this mountain ridge, recognisable by their deeply 'fingered' wings raised stiffly in a shallow 'V' above the body. The area also hosts **Bonelli's eagle** and **long-legged buzzards**, as well as both Peregrine and Eleanora's falcon. Rare and endemic plants include the *Erysimum naxense*—a yellow-flowered, upland cress—and 'hare's ear', *Bupleurum aira*, both of which grow on the upper screes of the ridge. The *Galanthus ikariae* snowdrop, found only in a few of the Aegean islands, also can be seen here at the higher altitudes when it flowers in March.

# THE TOWER OF HEIMAROS AND THE SOUTH COAST

(*From Filoti (20km) a road branches west then south to the coast at Kaladós, which lies at a distance of 24km to its south (44km from Chora). The same road must be taken to return, and there are no fuel facilities en route.*)

This is perhaps the island's most scenic stretch of road, beginning in the well-watered and protected valley of Ariés, populated with oak trees of great age and magnitude. There are Byzantine churches scattered amongst the trees and fields. Of greatest interest is the **Panaghia Arión (Y)**, a delightful, ruined 11th century church in a bucolic setting (east of road, 1.7km after initial junction at Filoti; path doubles back to church in middle of field). The entrance is framed by a finely carved Byzantine, marble lintel; elsewhere (by the doorway) ancient blocks have been incorporated. Thirteenth century paintings survive on the outside of the west wall, formerly enclosed by a (now ruined) domed narthex. Further along the main road, the churches of Aghios Anastasia (2.2km) and Aghios Eustathios (3km) at Mikraria, are also probably 11th century, but do not show paintings in the interiors; in the corners of the cupola of the latter, immured 'acoustic' pots are visible.

After crossing a **panoramic watershed**, the Hellenistic
*****Tower of Heimaros** (33.5km), standing to a height of
over 15m, appears on a low ridge with sweeping views
both to east and south.

The impressive circular tower is comparable in its good state
of preservation with the Hellenistic towers at Aghios Petros
on Andros and at Drakanon on Ikaria. The courses of rectangular masonry, shaped perfectly to the curve of the building, are thinner and finer here than at either of the other two
towers: they would suggest a date of the late 4th century BC.
To the right of the door as you enter, an area of masonry
is missing, and shows how the tower was constructed with
both an inner and outer shell. The upper wooden floors
were reached by a spiral, stone staircase.

The tower was the centre of a large **complex of agricultural buildings** of the same (Hellenistic) period, as is shown
by the extensive ruins to its west and southeast: querns, oil-
press stones, sedimentation, filtration and settling tanks,
etc. can all be seen, pointing to an installation of impressive
scale. There are over a dozen separate chambers dedicated to
different agricultural functions.

**Two early Byzantine churches**, on the foundations of
an Early Christian basilica, have been built into a corner
of the enceinte to the east of the tower. The north church,

dedicated to the Zoodochos Pigi, has fragments of an Early
Christian templon screen to the right of its altar, bearing the
words: ΦΩΣ—ΖΟΗ, 'Light, Life'. In the exterior of its west
wall, a shaped block from the tower has been incorporated,
and bears the ancient mason's marks in its top right corner:
'Τ Σ Μ'.

At 37km, a turning leads south to **Spedos**, site of the Early
Cycladic cemetery which has given its name to one of the
most prominent styles of marble figurine. At 38km, at
'Pirniá tis Farlas', the road makes a final descent by hair-
pin bends. On the hill to the right is the church of **Aghios
Ioannis Theologos Kaminos** (**Z**), partially hidden in the
trees: this is also built on the site of an Early Christian
Basilica.

The road descends beside a torrent bed, thick with oleander and reeds, to the shore at **Kaladós** (44km), looking
across to the island of Herakleia. The shore, today, basks
in sunny ignorance of the designs which developers in
Athens have on its innocent tanquillity.

# PRACTICAL INFORMATION

843 00 02 **Naxos**: area 389 sq.km; perimeter 133km; resident population 17,357; max. altitude 999m. **Port Authority**: T. 22850 22300 & 23939. **Tourist information**: Zas Travel (T. 22850 23330, fax 23419)

## ACCESS

**By boat:** Naxos has on average two or three connections per day throughout the year to Piraeus, and one or two each day to Rafina; the services all take cars, and the journey time typically varies between 4.25 hours (*Hellenic Seaways Highspeed & NEL lines*) and 5.5 hours (*Blue Star Ferries*). Nearly all services stop at Paros en route. There are daily connections south to Ios and Santorini in the summer, either by ferry or *Flying Dolphin*: this reduces considerably in the winter to twice-weekly. The *Express Skopelitis* leaves Naxos at 3 pm every day for the Lesser Cyclades Islands, weather permitting. **By air:** Olympic Air currently runs one daily return flight from Athens to Naxos, with small craft only (c. 30 seats). The airport is 3.5km from Chora.

## LODGING

For its size and importance, Naxos is poorly provided with good accommodations, outside the resort hotels. The

**Chateau Zevgoli** in the heart of the bourgo is the most charming place in Naxos, although its name promises more than it delivers and the rooms are small and over-decorated (*T. 22850 25201, fax 25200*). The owner, Mrs Despina Kitini, also possesses a couple of spacious studio rooms up in the Kastro, which represent a good alternative: she can be found at the useful 'Naxos Information Center' which she manages, opposite the main ferry quay. **Karabatsi Studios**, at Aghia Anna offer friendly, family hospitality of utter simplicity, at a short distance from the Chora (*T. 22850 26440, www. dinanaxos.com*). Of the resort hotels, **Lianos Village** at Aghios Prokopios, is comfortable and unpretentious (*T.* *22850 26366, fax 26362, www. lianosvillage.com*).

## EATING

Of the myriad tavernas on the harbour front at Chora, the freshest fish and seafood is to be had at the minuscule, '**To Steki tou Valetta**', where excellent octopus and wine are served. Of quite different character—elegant and with some carefully designed dishes—is **Elli's** restaurant in the Grotta area of Chora. For beachside eating, just outside Chora, **Paradiso** at Aghia Anna has good food, served at tables under trees on the sands. One of the best of all fish restaurants on the island outside Chora is **Michalakos** at Moutsouna. For its setting by springs in the village of Ano Potamiá, the taverna **Pighi** is a joy—very popular with locals on Sundays. **Katsalis**, under the plane trees in Filoti, is also to be recommended. And for making a picnic from the best Naxiot wine and produce, the **Tziblakis** cheese shop on the main Papavasileiou Street in Chora is still excellent—even if in recent years the shop has become more self-conscious than before.

## FURTHER READING

Theodore Bent, *The Cyclades* (1885), reissued 2002 by Archaeopress, Oxford in the '3rd Guides' series; Giorgios Mastoropoulos, *Νάξος, το ἄλλο κάλλος*/Naxos: Byzantine Monuments, Athens, 1996, an excellent documentation of Byzantine Naxos.

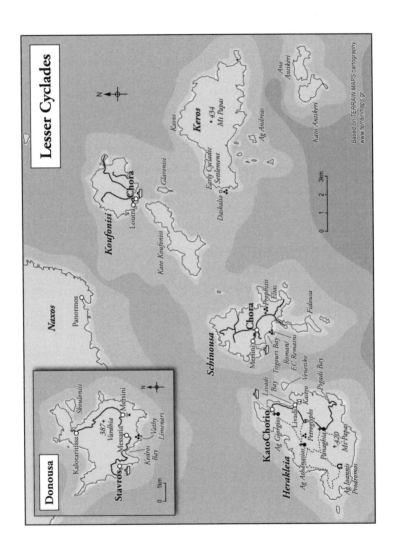

Lesser Cyclades

Based on TERRAIN MAPS cartography
www.terrainmaps.gr

Keros
+434 Mt Papas
Kavos
Ag Andreas
Early Cycladic Settlement
Daskalio
Glaronisi
Koufonisi
Loutro Chora
Kato Koufonisi

Ano Antikeri
Kato Antikeri

0  1  2  3km

Naxos
Panormos

Schinousa
Chora
Prophitis Elias
Mersini
Tsigouri Bay
Roman/E.C. Remains
Venetiko
Pigadi Bay
Fidousa

Herakleia
Kato Chorio
Ag Giorgios
Livadi Bay
Livadhi
Ag Athanasios
Panaghia
Pergophyli
Kastro
+420 Mt Papas
Ag Ioannis Prodromos

**Donousa**

Skopelitissa
Skoulonisi
Mersini
387 + Vardhia
Messaria
Stavros
Kedros Bay
Vathy
Limenari

0  1km

N

# THE LESSER CYCLADES

## (HERAKLEIA, SCHINOUSA, KOUFONISIA, KEROS, DONOUSA)

The waters of these islands are among the most protected in the Aegean, shielded from the North winds by the great bulk of Naxos. In the early morning especially, they can have the appearance of a lake in the middle of a ring of mountains and hills, with lacustrine mists sometimes enveloping the islands momentarily and hiding them from view. It was the proximity, intimacy and relative ease of communication that the islands offered which encouraged early man to settle here, and to flourish in a loose network of trading communities in the 3rd millennium BC. It is a unified and unthreatening seascape, offering the simultaneous boons of independence with community—remarkably similar to that of the Lesser Sporades to the north and east of Alonnisos, another area, uninhabited today, but which was in the vanguard of the earliest human settlement and commerce in the Aegean.

One of the principal differences between these and the Sporades islands however, is the astonishing productivity of worked marble objects found in this area: bowls,

goblets, and above all countless figurines, mostly of naked female forms. Almost one third of the Early Cycladic
figurines known today comes from the uninhabited island of Keros at the eastern edge of this group. Not all of
them were created in these islands by any means, but they
ended up here. Something of the enigmas raised by these
archaeological discoveries is discussed below.

Donousa, though close by, stands apart from the other
islands because its geography is different. It lies in the
full swell of the high sea, by contrast—often inaccessible because of the winds. Its importance was its strategic
position on one of the critical sea-crossings of Antiquity, between the western and eastern seaboards of the
Aegean, between the Cyclades and the western point of
Ikaria which was often used as the point of departure
from Asia Minor for the central Aegean. For this reason
its significant habitation is largely later than the Lesser
Cycladic islands, and dates from a time when the tech-
nology of sailing was more advanced. It is an island with
good sources of water and sheltered harbours, which
makes it harder to explain why its importance suddenly
faded, and that it should have had a flourishing settlement at Vathý Limenari in the 9th and 8th centuries,
but then apparently little of importance thereafter until
modern times.

Some of the islands in this group—Donousa and Herakleia—are havens of tranquillity; others—Schinousa
and Pano Koufonisi—are developing fast into centres
for visitors, attracted by their limpid waters and sandy
beaches which are ideal for snorkelling and for messing
about in boats. All of them offer a simplicity and intimacy
which contrasts markedly with the larger, surrounding islands.

### HISTORY

Human settlement has come and gone in these islands, and our knowledge of their history is consequently patchy. Until the first excavations in the
late 19th century, there was no awareness of the extraordinary human activity amongst these islands in
the 3rd millennium BC, and its importance for subsequent history. Some of the earliest lessons in the
handling and shaping of marble and the managing
of sea-vessels must have been learnt in these islands
and their waters. It has even been suggested that the
island of Keros was a central, sacred island—a sort of
proto-Delos—for the area in the Early Bronze Age.
The importance of these small Cycladic centres later
diminishes in a new world-order, polarised in the

Middle and Late Bronze Age between the cultural and commercial powerhouses first of Crete, then of Mycenaean Greece. During the Geometric period two relatively short-lived settlements on Donousa and Kato Koufonisi flourished. And then the lights virtually seem to go out. Keros, Ancient *Keria*, figured in Athenian tribute lists in 425 BC. Otherwise, little apart from the evidence of Hellenistic forts on Herakleia and Schinousa sheds light on these islands during the Classical and Hellenistic periods. The Romans had installations on them, but used them mostly as places of exile. A discreet Early Christian presence is evident on Schinousa, but the islands were too vulnerable to piracy and raiders for it to have had any continuity under Byzantine rule, which appears to have largely ignored the area. The archipelago became itself a base for pirates preying on the fertile shipping routes through the area. In the 18th century Schinousa and Herakleia belonged to the Chozoviotissa Monastery on Amorgos, which evidently derived supplies of timber from the former; the other islands were used as seasonal pasture by the inhabitants of Amorgos, except for Donousa which had a permanent population and paid a yearly tithe to the Sublime Porte during the period of Ottoman dominion.      In 1832 the islands were incorporated into the Greek State together with Naxos. Donousa had a growing population at the end of the 19th and in the early 20th century working the iron-ore mines on the island, which closed in 1938 at the outbreak of war. In 1941 the islands were occupied by the Italians and finally liberated from subsequent German occupation in 1944. Electricity was only brought to the archipelago in the mid 1980s.

## PRACTICAL INFORMATION

For Lodging and Eating see individual island entries.

### ACCESS

**By boat:** Lesser Cyclades: for such small islands, the ferry-services are frequent. The main-stay of communications is the F/B *Express Skopelitis* (with capacity for a small number of vehicles), which leaves Katapola on Amorgos daily in the early morning, and plies the route to Naxos, via Koufonisi, Schinousa, and Herakleia, returning (3pm) down the same line from Naxos: three days a week the route also includes Donousa. *Blue Star Ferries* follows the same route three times weekly, continuing directly to Piraeus from Naxos.

Donousa is less well-connected, with one weekly service to Piraeus (7 hrs: currently Mondays) with **Blue Star Ferries**, and three weekly connections to Naxos and Amorgos (Mon, Wed, Fri) with the *Express Skopelitis*.

## FURTHER READING

For a sense of the variety of readings and animated academic debate surrounding Early Cycladic figurines, see: Colin Renfrew, *The Cycladic Spirit: Masterpieces from the Nicholas Goulandris Collection*, New York, 1991; Pat Getz-Gentle, *Personal Styles in Early Cycladic Sculpture*, University of Wisconsin Press 2001; Cyprian Broodbank, *An Island Archaeology of the Early Cyclades*, Cambridge Uuniversity Press, 2002.

# HERAKLEIA

Herakleia is the largest of the Lesser Cyclades and is a momentary continuation above water of the chain of high mountains which runs from Naxos to Ios. It is the quietest and most beautiful of the islands in the group, with attractive beaches and mountain walks. There are two villages: Aghios Giorgios (the port) and Panaghiá (the 'chora'), which has no rooms and just one good taverna and bakery. Half way between the two is Kastro, the abandoned site of settlement in antiquity.

**Aghios Giorgios** is a deep sheltered port, backed with a tamarisk-shaded beach. Habitation climbs up to either side of a dry torrent-bed. The two principal churches are visible from the port—the patronal Aghios Giorgios in the centre, and the **Taxiarchis** at the south west end of the village. A column fragment, faintly inscribed with large, ancient lettering, stands beside its west door.

A 15 minute walk south brings you over a headland down to the beautiful **sandy bay of Livadi**. Dominating the bay from the south is the hill of **Kastro**, with the remains of habitation clearly visible on its ridge. This is an interesting site representing several layers of settlement from prehistoric to mediaeval times. Looking up at the north side of the hill from the shore at Livadi, a wall can be seen running across the summit. Its lowest course is constituted by the large irregular boulders of **prehistoric fortifications**. The principal Early Cycladic settlement on Herakleia is at the site of Aghios Mamas, inland to the south of here: Kastro may therefore have formed a subsidiary citadel, protecting the entrance from the sea. Today the top of the hill is an assemblage of collapsed stone houses, some with their well-built vaults still in place, and with cisterns and threshing floors visible. Habitation was only finally abandoned here in 1930. At the south end of the ridge where the buildings are best preserved, a quantity of large, cut, dark-coloured, rectangular blocks are included in the lower courses of masonry. These come from a 4th century BC, **Hellenistic structure** which stood here: the shapes of the blocks show that the building—probably a fortified tower—was not circular, but must have been rectangular in design, like the tower at Plaka in western Naxos. It is not evident where in the vicinity this darker stone was quarried. The area of foundations and shallow cut cisterns stretches some way farther to the south.

About 700m inland, the road to Panaghiá cuts across the old, paved mule-path at a sharp bend: there are many of these attractive *kalderimi*, or mule-paths, on the island. This one leads inland to the west towards the area of Aghios Athanasios—an abandoned community with a commanding view, now inhabited by only a couple of goat-herding families. Eight hundred metres west along this pathway (level with the first olive tree to the left of a scattered grove, and c. 100m before a T-junction) on some exposed, flat-surfaced rocks in the middle of the track, are two **prehistoric petroglyphs** in the forms of incised concentric rings. Although these are notoriously hard to date, they seem to belong to a common prehistoric visual vocabulary. The examples here are of remarkably similar size, technique and form to the rock-cut ring marks found in one of the most flourishing centres of distant Scotland in the same Neolithic and Bronze Age period—the Kilmartin Valley in Argyll.

The metalled road ends at **Panaghiá** (45 minutes by foot from Aighios Giorgos), which commands the most fertile slope in the island which stretches east down to the bay of Pigadi, with a distant view of the southern tip of Amorgos. The straggling main street is punctuated by the church complex of the Panaghia and Aghios Nektarios, and by two magnificent wind-sculpted Mediterranean pines. From the southern end of the village, the path to the **cave of Aghios Ioannis Prodromos**, leads down into the valley to the west, before rising steeply to round the shoulder of **Mount Pápas** (419 m). (*The walk is tough and there are no springs. Allow an hour and a half each way, and bring a powerful torch for the cave interior.*) The landscape, though bare and rocky, is exhilarating and panoramic. The two caves (*neither illuminated*) are set back in a deep cleft in the hillside. The wide-entranced cave to the left is a large chamber with some interesting stone formations inside. The entrance to the cave of Aghios Ioannis, to the right, is marked by a hanging bell. Entry is through a small hole on hands and knees, but the cave opens out immediately into a series of vast interconnecting chambers. Beyond the modern sanctuary-elements in the foreground, a clear path to the left side leads past stalactites, stalagmites and billowing calcareous encrustations, into the depths of the cave.

# PRACTICAL INFORMATION

843 00 **Herakleia:** area 18sq.km; perimeter 29km; resident population 133; max. altitude 419 m. **Port Authority:** T. 22850 22300 (Naxos). **Travel and information:** Gavalas Travel, T. 22850 71561, www.iraklia.gr

## LODGING

There is a wide selection of simple rooms on the island: prettiest of all are **Sunset Rooms**, at the top of the village of Aghios Giorgios (*T. 22850 71569, fax 71569, kovmaria@yahoo.gr*); the same owner keeps **Angelos Rooms** (same contact numbers) closer to the centre. Slightly more polished in facilities is **Anna's Place** (*T. 22850 74234, fax 71145*) also in Aghios Giorgios.

## EATING

**To Steki**, the taverna-cum-bakery in Panaghiá, serves the best home-cooking with fresh cheeses, fava and goat dishes on the menu. In Aghios Giorgios, **To Pefko** has good fare and an attractive position.

# SCHINOUSA

Where Herakleia's profile was mountainous, that of Schinousa is gentle, with low rolling hills and a deeply indented coastline of beetling promontories. Long gone is the island's rich vegetation that was able to supply the Chozoviótissa Monastery on Amorgos with timber, according to the monastery's archival records. A couple of large private compounds, fitted out with helipads, recreation areas and regimented tree-plantations strike a jarring note in the landscape, but in spite of sacrifices made to tourism it is remarkable that on Schinousa it is still possible to find some of the best fresh local wines and cheeses in the Cyclades. Schinousa prides itself on its split-peas for making *fava*, one of the most traditional of Cycladic dishes—courageously challenging the supremacy of Santorini.

The road from the attractive harbour of Mersini up to the Chora in the centre of the island (15 minutes by foot) is bordered by rock scarps shot through with grottos and declivities, some of which may have been burial places in origin but which were used throughout more recent centuries as hides for the local population of pirates. The Chora straggles to either side of an axial street. At the centre is the modern church of the *Eisodia tis Theotokou*

(Presentation of the Virgin); pieces of fluted and un-fluted ancient columns and Early Byzantine stone elements have been gathered in its courtyard. In the area immediately around the church, can be seen the outline of the former ***kastro***, whose quadrangle of houses still forms the core of the village.

Five hundred metres west of Chora is **Tsigouri Bay**, a wide beach of grey sands shaded by tamarisks. At the isthmus at the south end of the bay is a dense scatter of potsherds, both modern and ancient (amphora handles, cup bases, etc.), amongst an area of collapsed masonry which comes from a small-scale Roman and Early Christian presence here.

The island's fortified point was always the hill of **Prophitis Elias** (120m) which lies 1km to the south, by the left-hand branch of the road south from Chora. The southwest shoulder of the hill has the remains of prehistoric fortifications, with the plan of a rectangular bastion visible. Vestiges survive of the base of the wall along the north side. There are scatters of mediaeval pottery suggesting that the site was also used much later. Its position commands the south of the island and the waters between Amorgos and Naxos. Below the hill to the southeast are the ruins of a substantial, late-mediaeval '*pyrgos*'.

# PRACTICAL INFORMATION

843 00 **Schinousa**: area 8sq.km; perimeter 25km; resident population 197; max. altitude 134m. **Port Authority**: 22850 22300 (Naxos). **Travel and information**: Grispos Travel, 22850 71175, www.schinousa.gr

## LODGING

The most comfortable hotel, in a shaded position overlooking Tsigouri Bay, is **Grispos Villas** (*T. 22850 71930, fax 71176, www.grisposvillas-schinousa.com*); in Chora, **Christina's Apartments** provide self-catering comfort (*T. 22850 71922, or, in Athens, 210 993 1111*).

## EATING

The taverna *'**I Vengiera**' (*H Βεγγιέρα*) serves its own tangy *mizithra* cheese early in the year: it is capable of auto-locomotion if left on the plate too long. It has excellent local amber-coloured sea-salty wine on request, as well as good homemade *keftedakia* of meat and home-grown vegetables. This is a good place to sample the island's famous *fava*.

# KOUFONISIA
# (PANO KOUFONISI & KATO KOUFONISI)
# AND KEROS

The former character of the island—a remote but busy fishing community—has been transformed by intensive tourist and building development which is felt all the more pressingly since the island is small and has no notable geographical features. It is remarkable that a flat, waterless and shadeless island should be the object of such a boom, but the several beaches which lie mostly to the east of the port and town perhaps explain why. The setting of the island is also beautiful, in the calm waters between the mountains of Naxos to the north and of Keros to the south.

Something of the original nature of the village, built over the remains of a Hellenistic and Roman settlement, can still be felt in its winding paved main-street. Its focus is the church of **Aghios Giorgios**, which has in its courtyard a few fragments of early Christian carving and one ancient capital used as a fence post. The former port of the island was at **Loutra**, just to the west of the Chora, which still retains an active boatyard and has a quieter atmosphere. An Early Cycladic cemetery, being rapidly eroded by the sea, was excavated on the western side of the inlet; another was explored to the east of the Chora. Above the bay of Loutra stands a restored windmill and beyond it the church of **Aghios Nikolaos** in whose gateway and immediate surroundings several more carved marble elements, largely from an Early Christian structure, have been gathered together.

Across the water at a distance of less than a kilometre is **Kato Koufonisi**—uninhabited and with a more varied shore-line and relief than Pano Koufonisi. (*Excursion boats—see Prasinos Travel, T. 22850 71438—ply to and fro in the summer months, principally to the island's virgin beaches and to a seasonal taverna which opens there.*) Late Cycladic remains have been found on the island, with pottery showing strong Minoan and Mycenaean influence, and behind the wide sweep of Pori Bay a Late Geometric settlement has been identified. The island's grassy and sandy scrub, with a thick cover of thyme, is a favoured habitat for *Mesobuthus gibbosus*, the Mediterranean checkered scorpion. The island also supports several breeding pairs of **Eleanora's falcon**.

Across the water from Koufonisi is the island of **Keros** (*visits only with permit from the Greek Archaeological Service*) whose mountainous profile closes this 'inland sea' to the east. Keros is uninhabited and used mostly for goat-pasturing and bee-keeping. The island's fame rests on its integral role in the world of Early Cycladic culture and on the extraordinary quantity of finds of marble figurines and objects made, above all at the island's western extremity at Kavos, and at Daskalio, which though an islet now, was a rocky promontory of the main island in the Early Bronze Age.

## THE 'KEROS HOARD'

Between a quarter and a third of the existing body of known Cycladic marble figurines in the world today comes from one source on the island of Keros. This was first discovered in secret around 1958, and by the time that archaeology's most prominent student of Cycladic culture, Colin Renfrew, came to Keros in 1963 much of the material had already been looted and illegally exported, and the archaeological context of the finds irreparably disturbed. The looted pieces, which found their way into collections, private and public, around the world in the 1960s and 70s, have come to be known as the 'Keros hoard'. When in July 1990 a number of them, collected by Hans Erlenmayer of the University of Basel, were put on sale at Sotheby's in London, they became the object of a court injunction inspired by the Greek Government and of a public appeal by Professor Renfrew to Lord Gowrie, then chairman of the auction house, for the sale not to go ahead. It did in the end and over half of the pieces were purchased by the Goulandris Museum of Cycladic Art and are now on view in Athens.

The nature of the find presented many anomalies, however: previously such pieces had been found in graves by and large, but on Keros no cemetery with human remains had yet been found: only evidence of a Bronze Age settlement on the islet of Daskalio, opposite where the hoard had been located. The pieces were nearly all broken, and their fragmentary condition was generally ascribed to the looters. Colin Renfrew doubted this, however, and observing the lack of joinable fragments, as well as the weathered character of the fractured surfaces, hypothesised that they must have been deposited already in a broken condition. The variety of marble and pottery pieces furthermore suggested that they had been brought from sources on different islands to this one deposit on Keros. In 2006, excavations at the site of Daskalio-Kavos by Renfrew and Olga Philaniotou, unearthed a new, undisturbed deposit of pottery, rich in marble figurines and bowls coming from diverse origins. Once again the systematic breakages confirmed what Renfrew had suggested, namely that the material appeared to have been broken before being buried—a curious state of affairs with no parallel occurrences in the ancient world before or after. It seems therefore, that as early as 2,500 BC, an important ritual centre which may have functioned as a focus for the whole region was established on Keros—almost as if it were a 'sacred island' in the manner that Delos was to become in later history; and at this 'sanctuary' fragments of figurines and other objects, which had been broken either elsewhere or in a ritual at the site, were buried in large caches.

### The figurines

The beauty of the figurines, which date from the Early Bronze Age (c. 2800–2000 BC) and develop in style within that period, derives as much from the exquisite quality of their white, Naxiot marble, as from their workmanship. Vestiges of colour, suggest that a number of them were painted with facial features: normally almond-shaped eyes and eyebrows, but also hair, dotted patterns on the cheeks, and in some cases even a kind of diadem. Most, but not all, are female; most, but not all, have their arms folded in front of them—left arm above right. In most, but not all, the neck is slightly elongated, the face lyre-shaped, and the pose recumbent: even though we see them exhibited 'standing', the angle of the feet means that they could not stand, but instead lay, with the knees very slightly raised. This, together with the folded arms, might suggest a funerary purpose; but by no means all the figurines have been found in graves. Then there is the 'Keros enigma', of the ritual fracturing and dumping. In short, the meaning and purpose of these figurines are as elusive as their simplicity and homogeneity are appealing.

Two of the most striking finds from Keros are the 'musicians'—a standing flute-player and a seated harp-player (now in the National Museum, Athens), both found in a single grave. These alone are sufficient to show that we are looking at the very origins of a long tradition of Western sculpture in these anonymous artists of 4,500 years ago. Cycladic figurines mark the emergence of the basic techniques of cutting, drilling and polishing, which were to under-pin the greatest tradition of marble sculpture in the history of Western Art—the tradition which was to re-emerge in the grand figures of the Archaic *kouroi*, whose pose does not differ that greatly. As with the Archaic pieces, the Cycladic figurines were designed according to a simple canon of proportions, and a strong binding tradition, passed from generation to generation of sculptor, governed the harmony of their angles and forms. Henry Moore commented that it was as if the sculptors 'couldn't go wrong, but arrived at a result that was inevitable from the very beginning'.

# PRACTICAL INFORMATION

843 00 **Koufonisi:** area 5sq.km; perimeter 17km; resident population 376; max. altitude 114m. **Port Authority:** 22850 22300 (Naxos). **Travel and information:** Prasinos Travel, T. 22850 71438, fax 74249, www.koufonisia.gr.

## LODGING

An unusual solution for lodging on Koufonisi is **Villa Windmill**, a restored, thatched windmill in Loutra which accommodates one family only (*T. 22850 74294, or mob. 6944 527 607*). Of the many good, rental-room possibilities on the island, **Anna's Rooms** (*T. 22850 71061*) are new, welcoming and also situated in the quieter area of Loutra.

## EATING

**Lefteris** has a pleasing setting, set back from the Megali Ammos; and **Kapetan Nikolas** (Loutra) is good for fresh fish and seafood, and has rooms for rent above.

# DONOUSA

Donousa lies separated from the other Lesser Cyclades to the north, in an isolated position 15km from the east coast of Naxos: the next landfall to the east is Patmos (50km) or, to the northeast, Ikaria (45km) across open seas. It is a mountainous island for its small size, delightful and peaceful to visit, with a number of fine sandy bays and depths of turquoise water around its shores. The island has three good springs, and early in the year it is remarkably green. Aeneas speeds by Donousa after leaving Delos at the start of his voyage from Troy to Italy, and Virgil refers to the island as 'green': ('*Bacchatamque iugis Naxon viridemque Donusa/… legimus*', *Aeneid* III, 125). Other than to a poet, Donousa impinged on the Roman consciousness merely as a place of exile.

The Chora is well-kept with plenty of flowering shrubs and trees; there have not been dislocated rashes of building on the island, and outside the port area there is a just mixture of old and new buildings scattered in the landscape. The majority of the island is wild and scrub-covered. Chora, properly called **Stavrós**, centres around a sheltered bay and beach, with a well-watered '*kambos*' area behind. The belfry of the Church of the Stavrós

(Holy Cross) incorporates an antique capital and column: the church was built in 1902 and its interior is decorated with modern Byzantine paintings of some quality from the same period—a graceful *Nativity*, and *Miraculous Draught of Fishes*.

From the road which circles round Chora to the north, tracks lead up into the centre of the island where the iron-ore mines were; these were an important source of employment for the islanders until they were closed at the outbreak of World War II. To the east, the main surfaced road passes below the church of the Panaghia and then rises above **Kedros Bay** with one of the island's most attractive beaches (*steps down to the sands*). The road continues to climb to Messariá, a settlement of a few stone houses: from the bend below the village, a track leads downhill towards the site of **Vathý Limenári**, an important Geometric fortified settlement which flourished in the 9th and 8th centuries BC. The variety of pottery found here shows that this was a trading station within a network of routes connecting the other Cycladic islands, Euboea and Attica with the Dodecanese; the settlement does not seem to have survived into Classical times, however. The site is difficult to locate: a promontory crowned by a defunct windmill is clearly visible; the next shoulder to the east has a half-deserted house on its saddle, and the site extends to the east of this building. The ditches excavated by the archaeologists to reveal the fortification walls can be seen, with the settlement's water-source just below. In spring the hillsides are covered with colonies of squills and wild orchids (mostly *Anacamptis pyramidalis*).

As it climbs higher the road comes to **Mersini**, a panoramic village of dry-stone houses. From the church of Aghia Sophia on the shoulder of the hill, a path leads down to the generous **spring** below, which rises beside plane-trees and gives life to thick stands of broom and cane, which burst upon an otherwise rocky mountainside. The water is good and abundant, but not particularly sweet. From Mersini the road turns north, high above the island's most dramatic shoreline of rocks and promontories. Though treeless now, the hillside was once intensively terraced for cultivation. The road ends at **Kalotarítissa**, a tiny village set behind a jetty and a beautiful configuration of bays, with the island of Skoulonisi lying just offshore.

### DONOUSA: 9 AUGUST 1914

In the course of one of the most dramatic episodes in the turmoil at the outbreak of war in Europe in 1914, two German battle cruisers *SMS Goeben* and *Breslau*, under the command of Rear Admiral Wilhelm Souchon, effected a crucial refuelling with coal in the Bay of Stavros on Donousa on 9 August, on their way to the Dardanelles from the Central Mediterranean, while under pursuit by the British Navy. The Royal Navy failed to intercept them on Donousa. They escaped all subsequent interception and arrived at Istanbul. The strategic consequence of this was the forcing of the hand of the Ottoman Empire—thitherto neutral—into joining the war on the side of the Central Powers. It was widely seen as a bungled exercise, which subsequently resulted in the recalling of two Royal Naval admirals, one of whom was court-martialled. The failure, however, may have been partially the consequence of faulty and contradictory communications in the febrile and rapidly shifting state of events in the opening days of the First World War. It has been estimated that the consequences of the Ottoman Empire entering the war, precipitated by this event, led to the prolongation of conflict perhaps by as much as two years—two years of the costliest fighting in history in terms of human sacrifice and suffering. The consequence for Turkey itself of not remaining neutral was the dismemberment of its empire by the victorious allies at the end of the war, and the countless problems attendant on that fact which still plague our world today. Churchill, who had been First Lord of the Admiralty at the time, looking back at the event, wrote that the two German ships which the Royal Navy had failed to stop and intercept at Donousa, brought 'more slaughter, more misery and more ruin than has ever before been borne within the compass of a ship'.

# PRACTICAL INFORMATION

843 00 **Donousa:** area 13sq.km; perimeter 31km; resident population 166; max. altitude 383 m. **Port Authority:** T. 22850 22300 (Naxos). **Travel and information:** Sigalas Travel, T. 22850 51604 & 51570, fax 51607, www.donoussa.info

## LODGING

The island has limited accommodation on offer: the best is represented by the rooms (and adjoining taverna) of **To Iliovasilema** (*T. 22850 51570*), to the east of the harbour.

## EATING

The taverna **Tzi-Tzi** is memorable for its magnificent panoramic position above the springs at Mersini, 3km east of the port at Stavrós.

# GLOSSARY OF TECHNICAL TERMS

*a secco*—colour applied onto the dry surface of a wall-painting rather than into wet plaster

*aedicule*—a niche, or small shrine, often with architectural frame

*aghiasma*—a place where there is holy water; a holy spring

*ambo*—the pulpit or lectern of an Early Christian church

*antae*—square pilasters or projections of side-walls which frame an entrance or portico

*apotropaic*—having the power to turn away evil

**Archaic period**—the 7th and 6th centuries BC

*cella*—the interior space of a temple (cp. *naos*)

*chryselephantine*—fashioned from a combination of gold and ivory

*clerurchy*—an imposed colony in which settlers keep the citizenship of their home city

*crepis*—the platform of a temple

*Deësis*—the word means 'prayer', but refers to a pictorial composition in icons which became current after the 11th century, in which the figure of Christ is flanked by interceding Saints, most commonly Mary and St John the Baptist

*dipteral*—of a temple, with a peristyle of double rows of columns

*dromos*—an entrance passage or axial approach to a tomb or building

*exedra*—an architectural protrusion or a free-standing structure of semicircular form

'**free cruciform plan**'—design of a church in which the lateral arms protrude freely from the body of the building (cp. 'inscribed cross plan' below)

**Geometric period**—the 10th–late 8th centuries BC

**Hellenistic period**—era of, and after, the campaigns of Alexander the Great, c. 330–c. 150 BC

*hesychast*—one who practices spiritual quietism and retreat (a religious practice that arose on Mount Athos in the 14th century)

*in antis*—(of columns) set between projecting side-walls or wings (antae) of a building

'**inscribed cross plan**' or 'cross-in-square'—design of a church whose exterior is square, but within which the interior space is articulated in the shape of a cross

*isodomic*—(of masonry) constructed in parallel courses of neatly-cut rectangular blocks

**kambos**—any fertile area near a settlement used for food-cultivation

*kouros*—the statue of a nude, male figure

*martyrion*—a building (mostly circular) which enshrines the remains of a holy person, similar to, and deriving from, the pagan heroön

*naos*—the central interior area of a Byzantine church or the inside chamber of a pagan temple

*narthex*—the entrance vestibule of a Byzantine church, often running the width of the building

*opus sectile*—floor or wall decoration created from cut and inlaid polychrome stones

*peripteral*—of a temple which is surrounded by a peristyle of columns

*phialostomia*—hollow terracotta tubes or mouths with crimped sides, immured in the masonry of Byzantine buildings for decorative purposes and to ventilate the walls

*piano nobile*—the principal upper floor of an important residence

**poros stone**—any soft limestone of porous composition used for construction

*pronaos*—the front vestibule of a temple, preceding the *naos*

*propylaia*—the monumental gateway at the entrance to a sanctuary or street

*pro-style*—(of a building) with an entrance or portico of free-standing columns *socle*—a (slightly protruding) ledge forming the foundation of a wall

**synthronon**—the rising, concentric rings of seats for the clergy in the apse of a church

*templon*—the screen in a church which closes off the sanctuary

*tesserae*—the small pieces of coloured stone or glass-paste which compose a mosaic

*tetramorphs*—the pictorial symbols of the four Evangelists (Matthew, a man; Mark, a lion; Luke, a bull; and John, an eagle)

*thesmophoreion*—a place for the ritual worship of Demeter, frequented by women

# INDEX

Nigel McGilchrist is an art historian who has lived in the Mediterranean—Italy, Greece and Turkey—for over 30 years, working for a period for the Italian Ministry of Arts and then for six years as Director of the Anglo-Italian Institute in Rome. He has taught at the University of Rome, for the University of Massachusetts, and was for seven years Dean of European Studies for a consortium of American universities. He lectures widely in art and archaeology at museums and institutions in Europe and the United States, and lives near Orvieto.